CLOUD EMPOWERMENT

Demystifying Cloud Technology for Business Professionals

SUNIL DAS

Demystifying Cloud Technology for Business Professionals

Copyright © 2023 **Sunil Das.**

(Cover Page Design: KOMAL DAS)

All rights reserved.

ISBN: 9798860538436

Disclaimer

The purpose of **Cloud Empowerment: Demystifying Cloud Technology for Business Professionals**. is to provide general guidance and insights into the world of cloud technology and its potential benefits for businesses. The author and publisher have made reasonable efforts to ensure the accuracy and completeness of the information presented herein, but we make no express or implied representations or warranties about the completeness, accuracy, reliability, suitability, or availability of the information contained in this book. You use such information entirely at your own risk.

Professional Advice

This book is not intended to replace professional advice or consultation in areas such as law, finance, or technology. Readers are encouraged to seek qualified professional advice and recommendations for advice and recommendations tailored to their specific circumstances and needs.

Technological and industrial advancements

The field of cloud technology has been rapidly evolving since the publication of this book, and new developments, innovations, and best practices may have emerged. The author and publisher accept no responsibility for any errors, omissions, or outdated information. For the most up-to-date information, readers must stay current with industry trends and consult the most recent sources and experts.

Limitation of Liability

The author and publisher are not liable for any direct, indirect, special, incidental, or consequential damages arising from the use of this book's information. This includes, but is not limited to, data loss, loss of profits, and any other damages, whether or not they were anticipated.

Websites and Resources Provided by Others

Corrections and recommendations

While the author and publisher have made every effort to ensure the accuracy of this book, feedback and corrections are always welcome. If you believe any of the information in this book is incorrect or needs to be updated, please contact us at the address listed in the book, and we will take your suggestions into consideration for future editions.

Acknowledgment

The author would like to thank the cloud technology experts and professionals whose insights and knowledge influenced the content of this book.

By using this book, you agree to accept and abide by the terms and conditions outlined in this disclaimer. You are solely responsible for any actions or decisions you take in response to the information in this book.

Sunil Das.

Author

CLOUD EMPOWERMENT

Table of Contents

CLOUD EMPOWERMENT

Introduction

Cloud Empowerment: Demystifying Cloud Technology for Business Professionals now available! The title implies that the book's goal is to provide business employees with the knowledge and skills they need to effectively use cloud technology for professional tasks and projects. It implies that the book will provide valuable insights and practical guidance for leveraging the cloud's benefits in a business context. It is a Business Professional's Guide to Mastering Cloud Technology.

Cloud technology has emerged as a game changer in today's ever-changing business landscape. It has transformed the way businesses operate, allowing for greater flexibility, scalability, and innovation. You understand the importance of staying ahead of the curve as a business professional, and this book is your road map to harnessing the power of the cloud to drive success.

With the rapid development of developing cloud technology, non-tech business people from a range of industries are definitely feeling a surge of both promise and confusion. Although the cloud has many benefits, it also has a number of drawbacks and inconveniences that cannot be overlooked. The learning curve is one of the biggest problems; adjusting to new cloud-based tools and platforms may be scary, making many professionals feel like they are traveling through uncharted territory. Data breaches and privacy concerns are still at the top of peoples' minds as security worries. It can be difficult to integrate current systems or even select the best cloud solutions for their unique needs due to the complexity of cloud infrastructures. Additionally, the frequently unforeseen expenditures linked to cloud services can put a burden on finances and cause concerns about the return on investment. In conclusion, even though the cloud has the power to alter enterprises, non-tech professionals are forced to deal with a variety of problems that, in this rapidly changing tech-driven economy, need their attention and comprehension.

This book is the culmination of my love of technology and my commitment to making the complex world of cloud computing accessible to professionals like you. I've seen the transformative impact of cloud technology on businesses of all sizes and industries over the years. I've seen businesses use the cloud to streamline operations, increase agility, and discover new growth opportunities.

Cloud Empowerment is more than just a technical manual. It's a practical guide for business leaders, managers, entrepreneurs, and anyone else who wants to confidently navigate the cloud. This book is designed to meet you where you are, whether you are a seasoned executive or just starting out in the world of cloud technology.

These pages provide a thorough examination of cloud concepts, best practices, and real-world case studies. I've worked hard to make this book understandable, informative, and actionable. You will not be overwhelmed by technical jargon or abstract theory. Instead, you'll gain a firm grasp on how cloud technology can be used to improve business outcomes.

WHAT YOU CAN EXPECT TO FIND HERE

Cloud Technology's Foundations: We'll begin by laying a solid foundation by deconstructing the core concepts and models that underpin cloud computing.

Selecting the Best Cloud Strategy: I'll walk you through the process of determining which cloud approach is best for your organization, whether public, private, or hybrid.

Getting the Most Out of the Cloud: Learn how to use cloud management and governance to optimize your cloud resources, reduce costs, and increase efficiency.

Compliance and security: Learn how to keep your data and operations safe in the cloud while adhering to industry standards and regulations.

Scaling for Expansion: Investigate strategies for scaling your cloud infrastructure as your company expands, ensuring that your technology can keep up with your ambitions.

Best Practices and Case Studies: Real-world examples and practical advice from industry experts will motivate and inform you on your cloud journey.

My goal throughout this book is to provide you with the knowledge and confidence you need to make informed decisions about cloud technology. I want you to see the cloud as a powerful tool for achieving your business goals, whether they are to increase profitability, enter new markets, or drive innovation.

Remember that the cloud is a journey, not a destination. It's a journey I'm looking forward to sharing with you through the pages of this book. You'll be better equipped to leverage the cloud's transformative potential for your organization as you read, reflect, and apply the insights you gain.

Thank you for entrusting your future to **Cloud Empowerment**. I hope you find this book informative, entertaining, and ultimately useful in your quest to master cloud technology.

Good luck to your journey of cloud empowerment!

Author:

Sunil Das.

Chapter 1
Introduction to Cloud Computing

1.1 WHAT IS CLOUD COMPUTING?

DEFINITION AND BACKGROUND:

The delivery of computing services, such as servers, storage, databases, networking, software, analytics, and intelligence, over the internet (the "cloud") enables faster innovation, adaptable resources, and scale economies. Rather than having to own and maintain physical hardware and software, it enables businesses and individuals to access and use a shared pool of computing resources.

IMPORTANT HISTORICAL MILESTONES

1960s–1970s the evolution of utility computing and timesharing systems can be linked to the earliest concepts of cloud computing. Cloud computing was made possible by IBM mainframes and the introduction of virtualization.

The Internet Boom of the 1990s the foundation for remote access to computing and data storage was set by the widespread adoption of the internet.

Early 2000s - Web services start to take off: Launched in 2002, Amazon Web Services (AWS) is frequently regarded as the father of contemporary cloud computing. The foundation for the larger cloud market was laid by its initial provision of basic services like computing and storage.

Mid-2000s - Rise of SaaS: SaaS platforms like Salesforce and Google Apps became well-known for providing applications through web browsers.

Late 2000s - Spread of Cloud Providers: Microsoft Azure, Google Cloud Platform, and other cloud providers entered the market, enhancing the variety of cloud services accessible.

2010s - Cloud Domination: Cloud computing became the accepted norm for IT services and infrastructure. From platforms and applications to infrastructure, the term "cloud" started to refer to a broad range of services.

CLOUD COMPUTING ADVANTAGES INCLUDE:

Cost Effectiveness: Using the cloud eliminates the need for a large upfront hardware investment and lowers ongoing operational costs. A pay-as-you-go model charges you according to your usage.

Scalability: Depending on demand, cloud services can scale up or down, ensuring that you always have the right resources on hand without over-provisioning.

Flexibility and Agility: Cloud resources can be provisioned quickly, enabling quick application experimentation, development, and deployment.

Accessibility: Because cloud services are available from anywhere with an internet connection, they make remote work and international collaboration possible.

Availability and Reliability: Top cloud service providers offer dependable infrastructure with high availability and redundancy, lowering the risk of downtime.

Security: Cloud providers heavily invest in security measures, frequently going above and beyond what individual organizations can accomplish. They provide equipment and services for compliance, identity and access management, and encryption.

Automated Updates: Cloud service providers take care of infrastructure upkeep and software updates, making sure that your systems are using the most recent security updates and features.

Environmental Benefits: Cloud data centers frequently use less energy than conventional on-premises data centers, which lowers their carbon footprints.

Global Reach: Cloud service providers have data centers located across a variety of geographical areas, enabling redundancy and global reach.

Innovation: Cloud service providers frequently launch new products and innovations, giving businesses access to cutting-edge tools without making significant initial outlays.

Cloud computing has transformed the IT industry by giving businesses and individuals a scalable and affordable platform to innovate and grow without having to worry about managing complicated infrastructure. In today's technological ecosystems, it has become crucial.

1.2. CLOUD SERVICE MODELS

Different service models are available with cloud computing, and these models specify how cloud resources and services are managed and delivered. Different user and organizational needs and levels of control are catered for by these models.

- **Infrastructure as a Service (IaaS)**
- **Platform as a Service (PaaS)**
- **Software as a Service (SaaS)**
- **Function as a Service (FaaS)**

Each of these cloud service models offers distinct advantages and is suitable for different scenarios. Organizations often use a combination of these models to meet their specific needs and optimize resource utilization. An overview of the four main cloud service models is provided below.

IAAS: INFRASTRUCTURE AS A SERVICE

IaaS is a type of cloud service that uses the internet to deliver virtualized computing resources. In essence, it provides virtual machines, storage, and networking—the basic building blocks of IT infrastructure—as a service.

IMPORTANT TRAITS:

- **Virtualization:** To create and manage virtualized computing resources, IaaS heavily relies on virtualization technology.
- **Scalability:** Users can adjust resource levels up or down in response to demand, only paying for what they actually use.
- **Self-Service:** Through web interfaces or APIs, users can provision and manage their virtualized infrastructure.

  Examples include Google Compute Engine, Microsoft Azure Virtual Machines, and Amazon Web Services (AWS) EC2.

UC 1.1: HOSTING AND OVERSEEING VIRTUAL SERVERS IN A CLOUD INFRASTRUCTURE.

USE CASE DESCRIPTION:

- An organization uses infrastructure as a service to host and oversee virtual servers in a cloud infrastructure (IaaS). It emphasizes the key steps and benefits of using cloud services to host virtual servers.

ACTORS:

- The person in charge of configuring and managing virtual servers is a system administrator.
- Offering the infrastructure and IaaS platform is a cloud service provider.

PRECONDITIONS:

- The business utilizes a cloud service provider, and it is currently signed up with them (e.g., AWS, Azure, Google Cloud).
- For its virtual servers, the company has specified the hardware requirements (CPU, RAM, storage), operating system, and network configurations.

CLOUD EMPOWERMENT

FIRST FLOW

- The system administrator is chosen Provider of clouds: The system administrator logs into the cloud provider's management console.
- When choosing the cloud region or data center where they want to house virtual servers, they base their decision on factors like proximity to users or compliance requirements.
- The system administrator creates a virtual private cloud (VPC) or a similar network structure if a virtual network doesn't already exist.
- They set up subnets, security groups, and network settings to guarantee network isolation and security.
- establishing virtual servers
- The system administrator creates a new virtual server (virtual machine).
- They specify the server's operating system (such as Linux or Windows), as well as the security settings for the CPU, RAM, and storage allocation (firewall rules, SSH key, or RDP settings)
- if required, optional features like load balancing or auto-scaling.
- The virtual server is deployed by the cloud provider using the pre-set parameters.
- Following deployment, the System Administrator can access the server remotely via SSH or RDP.

MANAGEMENT AND CONFIGURATION:

- The system administrator of the virtual server installs and sets up all required software and services.
- They monitor server performance using tools provided by the cloud provider or by third-party monitoring programs.
- Regular upkeep and updates are done on the server to ensure its dependability and security.

- Postconditions include the organization's virtual servers being successfully hosted and operating in the cloud.
- The servers can be managed and maintained remotely by the system administrator.
- The organization benefits from the cloud service's scalability, flexibility, and affordability.

VARIOUS FLOWS:

- Materials Size If the organization's server requirements change, the system administrator can easily scale resources up or down without changing the server's IP address or configuration (for example, due to an increase in traffic).
- Unique Case Flows

RESOURCE CONSTRAINTS:

- If the cloud infrastructure runs into resource constraints, the system administrator may need to select a different region or change the resource requirements (for example, not enough CPU or RAM in the selected region).

BENEFITS:

- **Scalability:** Modifying server resources to meet changing demands is a simple process. Pay for only the resources you actually use.
- **Rapid Deployment:** Quickly provision and configure servers. Remotely control servers from any location with an internet connection.
- **High Availability:** Make use of the cloud provider's redundancy and failover features.

With the flexibility and scalability to handle their computing needs, this use case shows how businesses can efficiently host and manage virtual servers using cloud-based IaaS.

UC 1.2: DEVELOPING AND TESTING APPLICATIONS IN A CLOUD ENVIRONMENT

CLOUD EMPOWERMENT

USE CASE DESCRIPTION:

- This use case demonstrates how a development team can create and test applications in an effective and scalable way using cloud computing services. The main procedures and advantages of using cloud resources for application development and testing are described.

ACTORS:

- Development Team: Comprises developers, testers, and DevOps engineers responsible for application development and testing.
- Cloud Service Provider: Provides the cloud infrastructure and services needed for development and testing.

PRECONDITIONS:

- The development team has access to a cloud provider's platform (e.g., AWS, Azure, Google Cloud).
- Development and testing requirements, including codebase, test plans, and deployment strategies, are defined.

MAIN FLOW:

1. **Selecting the Development Environment:**
- The development team makes use of the cloud provider's development tools or console.
- They select an integrated development environment, a programming language, a development framework, and other factors when choosing a development environment (IDE).

2. **Code Development:**
- Developers write and collaborate on code using cloud-based development tools.
- Version control systems (e.g., Git) can be integrated for code management.

3. **Testing Environment Setup:**
- The team creates a dedicated testing environment in the cloud.

17

- This environment mirrors the production environment as closely as possible.
- Test data and scenarios are configured to simulate real-world usage.

4. **Continuous Integration (CI):**
- Developers integrate code changes into a shared repository.
- CI/CD pipelines, managed using cloud services or third-party tools, automatically build, test, and deploy the application to the testing environment.

5. **Testing and Quality Assurance:**
- Testers execute test cases and perform various testing types (e.g., unit testing, integration testing, performance testing).
- Automated testing scripts can be run using cloud-based testing tools.
- Test results and issues are tracked and managed in collaboration tools integrated with the cloud environment.

6. **Deployment and Staging:**
- Once testing is successful, the application can be staged for deployment to production.
- Cloud deployment tools ensure a seamless transition from the testing environment to production.

7. **Monitoring and Debugging:**
- The team uses cloud monitoring and logging tools to track application performance and identify issues.
- Developers can remotely debug applications using cloud-based debugging tools and logs.

POSTCONDITIONS:
- The application is thoroughly developed, tested, and ready for deployment to production.
- The development team has leveraged cloud resources for efficient collaboration and testing.
- The CI/CD pipeline is established for automating development, testing, and deployment workflows.

CLOUD EMPOWERMENT

ALTERNATIVE FLOWS:

- **Testing Failures:** If testing reveals issues, the development team can revise the code, re-run tests, and repeat the process until the application meets quality standards.

EXCEPTION FLOWS:

- **Resource Constraints:** If resource limitations occur within the cloud environment (e.g., insufficient computing power or storage), the team may need to adjust resource allocations or consider optimization strategies.

BENEFITS:

- **Scalability:** Easily scale resources up or down to accommodate development and testing needs.
- **Collaboration:** Enable remote collaboration among development and testing teams.
- **Automation:** Automate build, test, and deployment processes using CI/CD.
- **Cost Control:** Pay for resources used during development and testing, avoiding upfront hardware costs.
- **Rapid Development:** Speed up development cycles by quickly provisioning resources as needed.

This use case demonstrates how cloud computing can speed up the process of developing and testing applications, fostering efficiency, automation, and collaboration while lowering the burden of managing infrastructure.

UC 1.3: DISASTER RECOVERY AND BACKUP SOLUTIONS IN A CLOUD ENVIRONMENT

USE CASE DESCRIPTION:

- This use case demonstrates how a company uses cloud computing to implement disaster recovery (DR) and backup strategies, ensuring the availability of data and applications in the event of a catastrophe. It highlights the essential procedures and advantages of using cloud resources for data backup and disaster recovery.

ACTORS:

- IT Administrator: Responsible for setting up and managing the disaster recovery and backup solutions.
- Cloud Service Provider: Provides the cloud infrastructure and services for disaster recovery and backup.

PRECONDITIONS:

- The organization has active accounts with a cloud service provider (e.g., AWS, Azure, Google Cloud).
- Data to be backed up and protected, as well as recovery point objectives (RPO) and recovery time objectives (RTO), are defined.

MAIN FLOW:

1. **Selecting a Disaster Recovery Strategy:**
- The IT Administrator evaluates the organization's disaster recovery requirements, considering factors such as data criticality and budget constraints.
- They choose an appropriate disaster recovery strategy, which may include:
   - Backup and Restore: Regularly backing up data and applications to cloud storage for recovery.
   - Warm Standby: Maintaining a partially active duplicate environment in the cloud.
   - Pilot Light: Keeping essential systems and data in the cloud, ready for rapid scaling.
   - Multi-site: Deploying data and applications across multiple cloud regions for high availability.

2. **Setting Up Backup Policies:**
- The IT Administrator configures backup policies and schedules based on RPO and RTO requirements.

☁ Data and application backups can include databases, files, configurations, and virtual machine snapshots.

3. **Data Backup to the Cloud:**

☁ Backup processes are initiated to copy data and application states to cloud storage.

☁ Incremental backups are often used to reduce bandwidth and storage costs.

4. **Testing Backup and Recovery:**

☁ Periodic recovery tests are conducted to ensure data and applications can be successfully restored from backups.

☁ Recovery procedures and documentation are updated as needed.

5. **Disaster Recovery Planning:**

☁ The IT Administrator defines a clear plan for disaster recovery scenarios.

☁ This plan includes procedures for failover, DNS redirection, and communication with stakeholders.

6. **Continuous Monitoring:**

☁ Cloud monitoring tools are used to continuously monitor the health of the primary and backup environments.

☁ Alerts are configured to notify IT staff of any issues or anomalies.

7. **Disaster Response and Recovery:**

☁ In the event of a disaster, the IT Administrator initiates the disaster recovery plan, which may involve:

- Failing over to the backup environment.
- Redirecting traffic to the cloud-based systems.
- Restoring data and applications.
- Regularly updating stakeholders on the recovery progress.

POSTCONDITIONS:

- Data and applications are protected and can be recovered within defined RPO and RTO.
- The organization is prepared to respond to and recover from disasters effectively.
- Cloud-based disaster recovery solutions are continuously monitored and updated.

ALTERNATIVE FLOWS:

- Partial Failures: In cases of partial failures or data corruption, the IT Administrator initiates data restoration or recovery procedures based on the specific issue.

EXCEPTION FLOWS:

- Resource Constraints: If resource limitations occur within the cloud environment (e.g., insufficient storage or computing power), the IT Administrator may need to adjust resource allocations or consider optimizing backup and recovery processes.

BENEFITS:

- Data Protection: Safeguard critical data and applications from disasters.
- Scalability: Easily scale resources in the cloud to accommodate backup and recovery needs.
- Cost Efficiency: Pay for backup and recovery resources as used, without upfront hardware costs.
- Rapid Recovery: Reduce downtime by quickly restoring services in the cloud.
- Disaster Preparedness: Ensure the organization is well-prepared for unforeseen disasters.

With flexibility, scalability, and cost-effectiveness while protecting important data and applications, this use case shows how cloud computing can improve disaster recovery and backup solutions.

CLOUD EMPOWERMENT

UC1.4.: RUNNING SCALABLE WEB APPLICATIONS IN A CLOUD ENVIRONMENT

USE CASE DESCRIPTION:

- This use case describes how a company uses cloud computing services to set up and manage scalable web applications. It emphasizes the crucial actions and advantages of utilizing cloud resources to guarantee high performance and availability for web applications.

ACTORS:

- Web application development and deployment are the responsibilities of the development team, which is made up of developers, system administrators, and DevOps engineers.
- Scalable web applications can be run on the Cloud, thanks to Cloud service providers who offer the infrastructure and services required.

PRECONDITIONS:

- The company uses a cloud service provider and has an active account with them (e.g., AWS, Azure, Google Cloud).
- The deployment strategy, configurations, and codebase for the web application are specified.

PRIMARY FLOW

1. **How to Choose a Cloud Platform**
    - The development team assesses cloud platforms to determine which one best meets the needs of their application, taking into account elements like performance, scalability, cost, and geographic reach.
    - They set up a profile with the preferred cloud provider.
2. **Web application development and testing:**

Using cloud-based development tools, development environments, and version control systems, developers write and test the web application code.

- To guarantee code quality, continuous integration (CI) pipelines and automated testing are set up.
- Scalability is taken into consideration when designing the architecture of the web application, which makes use of cloud-native services for load balancing, auto-scaling, and distributed caching, as necessary.

3. **Setting Up a Deployment Environment:**
- The cloud deployment environment, which may include virtual servers, containers, or serverless functions, is configured by the development team.
- They set up the networking, storage, and database infrastructure required.
- Continuous Integration and Deployment (CI/CD): To automate the build, test, and deployment processes, CI/CD pipelines are set up.
- Code changes are submitted by developers to the repository, which starts automatic builds and deployments.

4. **Monitoring and scaling:**
- Application performance, resource usage, and user traffic are monitored using cloud monitoring tools.
- To ensure optimum performance, auto-scaling policies are set up to automatically adjust resources based on demand.

5. **High Availability:**
- To ensure high availability and fault tolerance, redundancy and failover mechanisms are put in place.
- To distribute traffic and lower the chance of downtime, multiple availability zones or regions may be used.

6. **Regular Maintenance and Updates:**
- The web application is regularly updated to include new features, security updates, and optimizations.

CLOUD EMPOWERMENT

- Tasks related to maintenance are carried out with little effect on users.

7. **Postconditions:**

- The web application has been successfully installed and is operating in a highly available and scalable fashion.
- For effective development, deployment, and maintenance, the development team makes use of cloud resources.
- When user traffic increases, the application automatically scales to accommodate it.

DIFFERENT FLOWS:

- **Scaling Triggers:** Auto-scaling triggers can be based on a variety of events, including a spike in traffic, a certain level of resource utilization, or a set schedule.

SPECIAL CASE FLOWS

- Resource Constraints: The development team may need to modify resource allocations, optimize application code, or think about scaling vertically if resource limitations arise in the cloud environment (for example, insufficient CPU or memory) (upgrading resources).

BENEFITS:

- **Scalability:** Easily increase or decrease resources to handle fluctuating user traffic. Price effectiveness Pay for resources as they are used rather than paying for hardware up front.
- **High Availability:** Assure that the web application can still be accessed even in the event of hardware failure or a spike in traffic.
- **Rapid Deployment:** By utilizing cloud-based resources and automation, development and deployment cycles can be sped up.

This use case demonstrates how cloud computing helps businesses run scalable web applications effectively by providing flexibility, scalability, and high availability while lowering the administrative burden associated with managing infrastructure.

PLATFORM AS A SERVICE (PAAS)

DEFINITION:

PaaS is a cloud service model that provides a platform and environment for developers to build, deploy, and manage applications without worrying about underlying infrastructure complexities. It includes tools and services for application development, middleware, and databases.

KEY CHARACTERISTICS:

- Abstraction of Infrastructure: PaaS abstracts infrastructure management, allowing developers to focus on code and applications.
- Automated Deployment: PaaS platforms typically offer automated deployment and scaling features.
- Development Tools: They provide development tools, frameworks, and services.
- Examples: Heroku, Google App Engine, Microsoft Azure App Service.

UC 1.5: WEB APPLICATION DEVELOPMENT AND HOSTING

Description:

This use case outlines how a development team leverages cloud resources to develop and host a web application, ensuring scalability, security, and high availability.

Actors:

Development Team, Cloud Service Provider, End Users

Preconditions:

- The development team has a concept and design for the web application.

CLOUD EMPOWERMENT

☁ The cloud service provider offers hosting services.

Main Flow:

1. **Development:**

   ☁ Developers use cloud-based development tools and environments to write and test the web application code.

   ☁ Version control is implemented to manage code changes.

2. **Web Application Setup:**

   ☁ The development team configures a cloud-based web hosting environment, selecting resources like virtual servers, storage, and network configurations.

   ☁ Security measures, including firewalls and SSL certificates, are implemented.

3. **Database Integration:**

   ☁ A cloud-based database is provisioned and integrated with the web application.

   ☁ Data schemas are defined, and initial data is populated.

4. **Continuous Integration and Deployment (CI/CD):**

   ☁ CI/CD pipelines are established using cloud-based tools to automate code integration, testing, and deployment.

   ☁ Developers commit code changes to the repository, triggering automated builds and deployments.

5. **Scaling and Monitoring:**

   ☁ Auto-scaling rules are set up to handle increased user traffic.

   ☁ Cloud monitoring tools are configured to track application performance, resource utilization, and user behavior.

6. **Regular Updates and Maintenance:**

   ☁ The development team regularly updates the web application to incorporate new features, security patches, and optimizations.

☁ Maintenance tasks are performed to ensure the application's reliability.

Postconditions:

☁ The web application is successfully developed, hosted, and accessible to end users.

☁ It is scalable, secure, and regularly maintained.

Alternative Flows:

☁ Scaling Events: Auto-scaling can be triggered by events like increased traffic or resource utilization.

☁ Database Failover: If the database experiences issues, failover to a backup database can be initiated.

Exception Flows:

☁ Resource Constraints: If resource limitations occur within the cloud environment (e.g., insufficient CPU or memory), the development team may need to adjust resource allocations or optimize application code.

Benefits:

☁ **Scalability:** Easily scale resources to accommodate changing user traffic.

☁ **Cost Efficiency:** Pay for resources as used, without the need for upfront hardware costs.

☁ **High Availability:** Ensure the web application remains accessible during traffic spikes or hardware failures.

☁ **Rapid Development:** Speed up development and deployment cycles by leveraging cloud-based resources and automation.

This use case illustrates how cloud computing enables organizations to efficiently develop and host web applications, offering flexibility, scalability, and high availability while reducing infrastructure management overhead.

UC 1.6: USE CASE TITLE: DATABASE MANAGEMENT AND DEVELOPMENT

CLOUD EMPOWERMENT

Description:

This use case outlines how an organization utilizes cloud resources to manage and develop a cloud-based database, ensuring data integrity, performance, and scalability.

Actors: Database Administrators, Development Team, Cloud Service Provider

Preconditions:

- The organization has data storage and processing needs.
- The cloud service provider offers database services.

Main Flow:

1. **Database Creation:**
   - Database administrators create a cloud-based database instance, selecting the database type (SQL, NoSQL) and configuration.
   - Security measures are set up during the database creation process.

2. **Data Import and Development:**
   - Data is imported into the database, and development teams access it for application development.
   - Data schemas are defined, and indexing is optimized for performance.

3. **Security and Access Control:**
   - Security measures such as authentication, authorization, and encryption are implemented to protect the database.
   - Access control policies are defined to restrict data access to authorized users.

4. **Scalability and Performance Optimization:**
   - Database scalability is managed by adjusting resource allocations (e.g., CPU, memory).
   - Indexing and query optimization are performed to ensure efficient data retrieval.

5. **Backup and Recovery:**

- Regular backups of the database are scheduled to protect against data loss.
- Disaster recovery plans are established, including backup restoration procedures.

Postconditions:

- The cloud-based database is successfully managed, secure, and optimized for performance.
- It serves as a reliable data source for applications.

Alternative Flows:

- Scaling: If data storage or processing needs increase, the database can be scaled horizontally or vertically, depending on requirements.
- Database Replication: Replication configurations can be set up for data redundancy and failover.

Exception Flows:

- Resource Constraints: If resource limitations occur within the cloud environment (e.g., insufficient CPU or memory), the database administrators may need to adjust resource allocations or optimize queries.

Benefits:

- **Data Security:** Protect sensitive data through authentication, authorization, and encryption.
- **Scalability:** Easily scale resources to accommodate growing data and user demands.
- **Cost Efficiency:** Pay for database resources as used, without the need for upfront hardware costs.
- **Data Integrity:** Ensure data remains consistent and available, with regular backups and disaster recovery plans.
- **Performance Optimization:** Improve database performance through indexing and query optimization.

CLOUD EMPOWERMENT

This use case demonstrates how cloud computing enables businesses to effectively manage and develop databases by providing scalable, secure, and affordable options for data processing and storage.

UC 1.7: USE CASE TITLE: IMPLEMENTING CI/CD FOR APPLICATION DEVELOPMENT

Description:

This use case outlines how a development team uses cloud-based CI/CD pipelines to automate the development, testing, and deployment of software applications.

Actors: Development Team, Cloud Service Provider, Testers

Preconditions:

- The development team has an application codebase.
- The cloud service provider offers CI/CD services.

Main Flow:

1. **CI/CD Pipeline Setup:**

- Developers configure a CI/CD pipeline using cloud-based CI/CD tools.
- The pipeline includes stages for code integration, testing, and deployment.

2. **Code Integration:**

- Developers commit code changes to a version control repository (e.g., Git).
- The CI/CD pipeline automatically triggers a build process when code changes are detected.

3. **Automated Testing:**

- The application undergoes automated testing, including unit tests, integration tests, and user acceptance tests.

Testing results are reported, allowing developers to identify and address issues.

4. Deployment:

Upon successful testing, the application is automatically deployed to a staging or production environment.

Deployment scripts and configurations are managed through the CI/CD pipeline.

5. Monitoring:

Cloud monitoring tools are configured to track application performance, resource utilization, and error rates in real-time.

Alerts are set up to notify the development team of issues.

6. Rollback and Versioning:

In case of deployment failures or issues, the CI/CD pipeline allows for automated rollbacks to a previous version.

Versioning ensures that multiple versions of the application can be managed.

Postconditions:

The CI/CD pipeline is successfully implemented, automating the development, testing, and deployment processes.

Applications are continuously integrated, tested, and deployed with high efficiency.

Alternative Flows:

Parallel Pipelines: Organizations may set up multiple parallel CI/CD pipelines to manage different application components or environments simultaneously.

Exception Flows:

Testing Failures: If automated tests fail, the development team is alerted, and they must address the issues before proceeding with deployment.

☁ Deployment Failures: In case of deployment failures, the CI/CD pipeline may trigger a rollback to a previous version, and the development team investigates and resolves the issue.

Benefits:

☁ **Automation:** Streamline the development and deployment process, reducing manual errors and saving time.

☁ **Continuous Integration:** Ensure that code changes are continuously integrated into the application, promoting collaboration among development teams.

☁ **Continuous Deployment:** Speed up the release process by automatically deploying new features and bug fixes.

☁ **Monitoring:** Proactively identify and address performance and stability issues in real-time.

☁ **Rollback:** Safeguard against deployment failures by easily rolling back to a previous working version.

By facilitating effective application development, testing, and deployment while ensuring a high level of automation and monitoring, this use case illustrates how cloud-based CI/CD pipelines can significantly improve the software development lifecycle.

UC 1.8: USE CASE TITLE: DEVELOPING AN IoT APPLICATION

Description

The development of an Internet of Things (IoT) application using cloud resources, including device connectivity, data processing, and real-time monitoring, is described in this use case.

Actors: IoT devices, a development team, and a cloud service provider.

Prerequisites.

☁ IoT devices are deployed and connected to the internet.

☁ The cloud service provider provides services for IoT connectivity and development.

Primary Flow

☁ Device registration and authentication: The cloud IoT platform registers IoT devices.

☁ Security and authentication protocols are used to make sure that only authorized devices can connect.

Data Ingestion and Processing:

☁ Data generated by IoT devices is ingested into the cloud IoT platform, such as sensor readings and telemetry data.

☁ To analyze and process incoming data in real-time, data processing pipelines are developed.

Real-time Monitoring and Control:

☁ To monitor IoT device data in real-time, developers create a web or mobile application.

☁ Control mechanisms have been put in place to enable users to control IoT devices remotely, such as turning them on and off.

Analytics and insights:

☁ To draw conclusions from IoT data, data analytics tools are used.

☁ Predictive maintenance, anomaly detection, optimization, and reporting are some examples of analytics.

Integration with External Services:

☁ To improve functionality and offer context, the IoT application can integrate with external services or APIs (such as weather data, third-party platforms).

Postconditions:

☁ The Internet of Things application has been successfully created and is running.

☁ IoT devices are networked, tracked, and offer insightful data.

☁ Remote users can communicate with IoT devices.

Different Flows:

CLOUD EMPOWERMENT

- Device management: The IoT application may have tools for setting up and controlling connected devices.
- Over-the-Air (OTA) Firmware Updates: The app may support OTA firmware updates for IoT devices.
- Support for Multiple Platforms: The IoT application can be accessed on a number of different platforms, including mobile apps, web browsers, and IoT dashboards.

Special Case Flows

- Device Interconnection Issues: The IoT application should notify users or offer troubleshooting advice if IoT devices encounter connectivity problems.
- Data Volume Handling: To handle exceptionally high data volumes from IoT devices effectively, data processing pipelines may need to be optimized.

Benefits:

- **Real-time monitoring:** Allows users to remotely monitor and manage IoT devices.
- **Data insights:** Use data analytics to get important insights for making decisions.
- **Automation:** To increase efficiency, automate responses and actions based on IoT data.
- **Scalability:** As the deployment expands, it can easily scale to accommodate more IoT devices.
- **Integration:** For improved functionality, seamlessly integrate with outside platforms and services.

This use case demonstrates how cloud computing resources can assist in the development of IoT applications through connectivity, data processing, real-time monitoring, and data-driven decision-making.

SOFTWARE AS A SERVICE (SAAS)

DEFINITION:

SaaS is a cloud service model where software applications are hosted and delivered over the internet on a subscription basis. Users access these applications through web browsers, and the software is maintained and updated by the service provider.

KEY CHARACTERISTICS:

- No Installation: Users don't need to install or maintain software on their local devices.
- Accessibility: SaaS applications are accessible from any device with internet access.
- Automatic Updates: Providers handle software updates and maintenance.

Examples: Salesforce, Google Workspace, Dropbox.

UC 1.9: USE CASE TITLE: EMAIL AND COLLABORATION TOOLS AS SAAS

Description:

This use case outlines how a medium-sized company utilizes SaaS-based email and collaboration tools to enhance communication and collaboration among its employees, regardless of their geographical locations.

Actors:

- Employees: Users within the organization who use the SaaS email and collaboration tools.
- SaaS Provider: The provider of the SaaS-based email and collaboration platform.

Preconditions:

- The company has subscribed to a SaaS-based email and collaboration service.

CLOUD EMPOWERMENT

- Users have been provided with individual accounts and access to the SaaS platform.

Main Flow:

1. **User Account Setup:**
- Employees are given access to the SaaS platform, where they set up their individual accounts.
- Each user customizes their profile, personal preferences, and notification settings.

2. **Email Communication:**
- Employees utilize the SaaS-based email service for sending and receiving emails.
- Features like inbox organization, spam filtering, and email search streamline email management.

3. **Calendar Management:**
- Users use the SaaS calendar tool to schedule meetings, appointments, and events.
- Calendar invites and reminders help manage time effectively.

4. **Document Collaboration:**
- Employees collaborate on documents in real-time using the SaaS-based collaboration suite.
- Features such as document sharing, simultaneous editing, and version control enhance teamwork.

5. **Video Conferencing:**
- Virtual meetings and video conferences are conducted using the SaaS platform's video conferencing tools.
- Additional features like screen sharing, chat, and recording contribute to effective remote collaboration.

6. **Task and Project Management:**

- Teams manage tasks and projects using the SaaS platform's project management tools.
- Task assignment, progress tracking, and project timelines improve project coordination.

7. **Mobile Access:**

- Users access the SaaS platform through mobile apps, ensuring they can collaborate and communicate while on the move.

Postconditions:

- Employees effectively use the SaaS email and collaboration tools for seamless communication, document collaboration, and project management.
- Collaboration and productivity within the company are enhanced, leading to improved outcomes and efficiency.
- Teams can work efficiently whether they are in the office, working remotely, or traveling.

Alternative Flows:

- **Guest Access:** The company may grant temporary access to external collaborators, such as clients, partners, or contractors, to specific collaboration spaces or documents.

Exception Flows:

- **Service Downtime:** In the rare event of service downtime or disruptions by the SaaS provider, employees may need to use alternative communication methods temporarily.

Benefits:

- **Cost-Efficiency:** Eliminate the need for on-premises email and collaboration server maintenance costs.
- **Scalability:** Easily adjust the number of user licenses as the company grows or changes.
- **Accessibility:** Access email and collaboration tools from any location or device with internet connectivity.
- **Collaboration:** Facilitate seamless collaboration and communication among dispersed teams.

CLOUD EMPOWERMENT

- **Productivity:** Streamline workflows and improve overall productivity with integrated tools.

This use case serves as an example of how SaaS-based email and collaboration tools can greatly improve internal communication, teamwork, and productivity while lowering the complexity of managing on-premises infrastructure.

UC 1.10: USE CASE TITLE: CUSTOMER RELATIONSHIP MANAGEMENT (CRM) SOFTWARE AS SAAS

Description:

The use case presented here shows how a sales and marketing team at a company uses SaaS-based CRM software to track sales leads, manage customer relationships, and enhance all-around customer engagement.

Actors:

- **Sales Team:** Users within the organization responsible for sales and customer interactions.
- **Marketing Team:** Users responsible for marketing campaigns and lead generation.
- **SaaS CRM Provider:** The provider of the SaaS-based CRM software.

Preconditions:

- The company has subscribed to a SaaS-based CRM service.
- Users have been granted access to the SaaS CRM platform.

Main Flow:

1. **User Access and Profile Setup:**
- Sales and marketing team members are granted access to the SaaS CRM platform.

- Each user sets up their profile, personalizes their dashboard, and configures notification preferences.

2. **Contact Management:**

- The sales team uses the CRM to manage customer and prospect contact information.
- Leads and contacts are added, edited, or archived within the CRM system.

3. **Sales Lead Tracking:**

- Sales representatives use the CRM to record and track sales leads, opportunities, and customer interactions.
- Lead statuses, notes, and communication history are maintained within the CRM.

4. **Marketing Campaigns:**

- The marketing team utilizes CRM data for targeted marketing campaigns.
- Campaigns are planned, executed, and tracked within the CRM platform.

5. **Customer Engagement:**

- Sales representatives engage with customers using CRM data to personalize interactions.
- Communication with customers occurs via email, phone, or other channels through CRM integration.

6. **Sales Pipeline Management:**

- The CRM platform provides a visual representation of the sales pipeline.
- Sales stages, probability, and revenue forecasts are tracked.

7. **Reporting and Analytics:**

- Both sales and marketing teams generate reports and analyze data within the CRM.
- Analytics help in measuring campaign effectiveness and sales performance.

CLOUD EMPOWERMENT

Postconditions:

- ☁ The sales and marketing teams effectively use the SaaS CRM software for managing customer relationships, tracking leads, and enhancing customer engagement.
- ☁ Improved lead conversion rates and customer satisfaction are observed.

Alternative Flows:

- ☁ **Integration:** The CRM platform can integrate with other business systems such as email, calendars, and marketing automation tools for enhanced functionality.

Exception Flows:

- ☁ **Service Downtime:** In the event of service downtime or disruptions by the SaaS CRM provider, users may need to rely on alternative methods for managing leads and customer interactions temporarily.

Benefits:

- ☁ **Accessibility:** Access the CRM system from anywhere with internet connectivity.
- ☁ **Collaboration:** Facilitate collaboration between sales and marketing teams by sharing real-time data.
- ☁ **Data Security:** Ensure customer data is stored securely and in compliance with data protection regulations.
- ☁ **Improved Customer Relationships:** Use CRM insights to personalize interactions and improve customer satisfaction.
- ☁ **Scalability:** Easily scale up or down as the organization's needs change, without the burden of managing on-premises CRM infrastructure.

This use case serves as an example of how SaaS-based CRM software can be instrumental in streamlining lead tracking, customer relationship management, and marketing initiatives within an organization, leading to more successful sales and enhanced customer engagement.

UC 1.11: USE CASE TITLE: DOCUMENT MANAGEMENT AND STORAGE AS SAAS

Description:

In order to centralize document storage, improve collaboration, and guarantee effective document access and management, this use case demonstrates how an organization uses SaaS-based document management and storage solutions.

Actors:

- Employees: Users within the organization responsible for document creation, editing, and access.
- SaaS DMS Provider: The provider of the SaaS-based Document Management System.

Preconditions:

- The organization has subscribed to a SaaS-based Document Management System.
- Users have been granted access to the SaaS DMS platform.

Main Flow:

1. **User Account Setup:**
- Employees are provided access to the SaaS DMS platform.
- Each user sets up their profile, personalizes their dashboard, and configures notification preferences.

2. **Document Upload and Storage:**
- Employees upload documents to the SaaS DMS platform.
- Documents can include text files, spreadsheets, presentations, images, and other file types.
- Document metadata (e.g., title, author, tags) is added for easy categorization and retrieval.

3. **Document Organization:**

CLOUD EMPOWERMENT

- Documents are organized into folders, projects, or categories within the SaaS DMS.
- Folder structures and access permissions are configured to ensure proper organization and security.

4. **Collaborative Editing:**

- Teams collaborate on documents in real-time using integrated editing tools.
- Changes made by one user are immediately visible to others, ensuring synchronized collaboration.

5. **Version Control:**

- The SaaS DMS automatically maintains version history for documents.
- Users can track changes, compare versions, and revert to previous versions if needed.

6. **Access Control:**

- Access to documents is controlled through role-based permissions.
- Users can be granted view-only, edit, or comment access, ensuring document security.

7. **Search and Retrieval:**

- Employees use search functionality to locate specific documents quickly.
- Search queries can be based on document content, metadata, or keywords.

8. **Document Sharing:**

- Users share documents with colleagues, clients, or external partners.
- Sharing options may include granting view or edit access, setting expiration dates, and restricting downloads.

Postconditions:

- The organization effectively uses the SaaS Document Management and Storage system to centralize document storage and enhance collaboration.
- Documents are easily accessible, securely stored, and well-organized.

Alternative Flows:

- Integration: The SaaS DMS can integrate with other business systems, such as email, CRM, or project management tools, to streamline document workflows.

Exception Flows:

- Service Downtime: In the event of service downtime or disruptions by the SaaS DMS provider, users may need to rely on local copies of documents temporarily.

Benefits:

- **Accessibility:** Access documents from anywhere with internet connectivity.
- **Collaboration:** Facilitate real-time collaborative editing and commenting on documents.
- **Security:** Ensure document security through access controls and encryption.
- **Compliance:** Support regulatory compliance with audit trails and version history.
- **Efficiency:** Streamline document storage, retrieval, and sharing processes.

The use case presented here shows how SaaS-based document management and storage solutions can greatly enhance document collaboration, accessibility, and organization within an organization while lowering the administrative burden associated with managing on-premises document storage systems.

UC 1.12 USE CASE TITLE: HUMAN RESOURCES AND PAYROLL MANAGEMENT AS SAAS

Description: This use case demonstrates how a medium-sized business manages HR procedures, employee data, and payroll operations effectively using SaaS-based human resources (HR) and payroll management software.

Actors:

- HR Administrators: Users responsible for HR tasks, including employee onboarding, data management, and payroll processing.
- Employees: Users whose personal and payroll information is managed within the SaaS system.
- SaaS HR and Payroll Provider: The provider of the SaaS-based HR and Payroll Management platform.

Preconditions:

- The company has subscribed to a SaaS-based HR and Payroll Management service.
- HR administrators and employees have been granted access to the SaaS platform.

Main Flow:

1. **User Account Setup:**
- HR administrators and employees are provided access to the SaaS HR and Payroll platform.
- Each user sets up their profile, configures personal information, and accesses relevant HR features.

2. **Employee Onboarding:**
- HR administrators use the SaaS system to initiate and streamline the onboarding process for new employees.

- New hires submit required documentation and information through the platform.

3. **Employee Data Management:**

- HR administrators maintain and update employee records within the SaaS platform.
- Changes to personal details, job roles, and benefits are recorded and tracked.

4. **Time and Attendance Tracking:**

- The SaaS platform includes time tracking features for employees to log their working hours, vacations, and sick leave.
- HR administrators review and approve time-off requests.

5. **Payroll Processing:**

- HR administrators use the SaaS platform to process payroll, calculating salaries, taxes, deductions, and benefits.
- Payroll reports are generated, and employees are paid through direct deposit or checks.

6. **Tax Compliance:**

- The SaaS platform automatically calculates and withholds payroll taxes, ensuring compliance with local and national tax regulations.
- Tax forms and reports are generated, and electronic filing is facilitated.

7. **Employee Self-Service:**

- Employees access the SaaS platform to view their pay stubs, tax forms, and personal information.
- They can update contact details, view company policies, and request time off.

8. **Reporting and Analytics:**

- HR administrators generate various reports and analytics using the SaaS system to monitor HR metrics, payroll expenses, and compliance.

CLOUD EMPOWERMENT

- Data-driven insights inform HR decision-making and strategic planning.

Postconditions:

- The company effectively uses the SaaS HR and Payroll Management system to automate HR processes, manage employee data, and process payroll accurately.
- Payroll compliance is maintained, and employees have easy access to their pay-related information.

Alternative Flows:

- Integration: The SaaS HR and Payroll platform can integrate with other systems, such as accounting software or benefits management platforms, for seamless data sharing.

Exception Flows:

- Service Downtime: In the event of service downtime or disruptions by the SaaS provider, HR administrators may need to employ backup payroll processing methods temporarily.

Benefits:

- Efficiency: Streamline HR and payroll processes, reducing administrative overhead.
- Accuracy: Minimize errors in payroll calculations and tax withholding.
- Compliance: Ensure adherence to tax regulations and labor laws.
- Employee Self-Service: Empower employees to manage their information and requests.
- Reporting: Access data-driven insights for informed HR decisions and cost management.

This use case shows how SaaS-based HR and payroll management software can greatly enhance HR efficiency, accuracy, and compliance within an organization while providing employees with self-service capabilities for accessing and managing their HR-related information.

FUNCTION AS A SERVICE (FAAS):

DEFINITION:

FaaS, also known as serverless computing, is a cloud service model that enables developers to run individual functions or units of code in response to events without managing servers. Developers write code to perform specific tasks (functions), and the cloud provider handles the underlying infrastructure.

KEY CHARACTERISTICS:

- Event-Driven: FaaS is event-driven, triggering functions in response to events like HTTP requests, database changes, or IoT sensor data.
- Automatic Scaling: The cloud provider automatically scales resources to handle function execution.
- Billing Model: Users are typically charged based on the number of function executions and resource usage.
- Examples: AWS Lambda, Azure Functions, Google Cloud Functions.

UC 1.13: USE CASE TITLE: REAL-TIME DATA PROCESSING WITH FAAS

Description:

This use case illustrates how a business uses FaaS to process incoming real-time data streams, carry out data transformations, and initiate prompt actions or notifications in response to particular data patterns or conditions.

Actors:

- **Data Sources:** Systems or devices that generate real-time data streams.

CLOUD EMPOWERMENT

- **FaaS Platform:** The provider of the Function as a Service platform.
- **Data Processing Functions:** Serverless functions deployed on the FaaS platform.
- **Action Handlers:** Components or systems that perform actions or send notifications based on processed data.

Preconditions:

- The company has access to a FaaS platform capable of handling real-time data processing.
- Data sources are configured to send data streams to the FaaS platform.

Main Flow:

1. **Function Deployment:**

- Data processing functions are developed and deployed on the FaaS platform.
- These functions subscribe to incoming data streams or events from data sources.

2. **Data Ingestion:**

- Real-time data streams from various sources, such as IoT devices, sensors, or web services, are ingested by the FaaS platform.

3. **Data Processing:**

- FaaS functions process incoming data streams in real-time.
- Data processing may involve filtering, aggregating, enriching, or transforming the data.

4. **Event Detection:**

- Data processing functions are designed to detect specific events or patterns in the data.
- For example, detecting anomalies in sensor readings or identifying critical threshold breaches.

5. **Immediate Actions:**
- When an event or condition of interest is detected, the FaaS function triggers immediate actions.
- Actions can include sending notifications, updating databases, or executing external APIs.

6. **Data Storage:**
- Processed data may be stored in a database for historical analysis or auditing purposes.
- FaaS functions can be configured to perform data archiving or cleanup tasks.

7. **Monitoring and Logging:**
- The FaaS platform provides monitoring and logging capabilities to track the execution of functions and the processing of data.
- Logs and metrics are used for debugging, performance optimization, and compliance.

Postconditions:
- The company effectively uses FaaS for real-time data processing, event detection, and immediate actions based on processed data.
- Critical events trigger timely responses or notifications.

Alternative Flows:
- Scale-Out: The FaaS platform automatically scales out the number of function instances to handle increased data volume or processing demands.

Exception Flows:
- Function Failure: If a function fails during processing, error-handling mechanisms are in place to log the issue and potentially trigger notifications for investigation.

Benefits:
- **Real-Time Insights:** Gain real-time insights from incoming data streams.

- **Scalability:** Automatically scale processing capacity based on data volume.
- **Cost Efficiency:** Pay only for the compute resources used during processing.
- **Responsiveness:** Trigger immediate actions or alerts in response to critical events.
- **Simplified Operations:** Eliminate server provisioning and management overhead.

This use case exemplifies how Function as a Service (FaaS) can be an effective real-time data processing solution, enabling businesses to process, examine, and react to incoming data streams quickly and effectively.

UC1.14: USE CASE TITLE: FAAS IN A MICROSERVICES ARCHITECTURE

Description:

This use case illustrates how a company adopts Function as a Service (FaaS) as part of its microservices architecture to achieve scalability, modularity, and cost efficiency in building and managing its software services.

Actors:

- Developers: Responsible for designing, developing, and deploying microservices and serverless functions.
- FaaS Platform: The provider of the Function as a Service platform.
- API Gateway: Manages API requests and routes them to the appropriate microservices or functions.
- Database: Stores data and interacts with microservices and functions.

Preconditions:

- The company has adopted a microservices architecture for its software.
- A FaaS platform is available for deploying serverless functions.

Main Flow:

1. **Microservices Development:**

- Developers design and implement various microservices to handle specific business functions or features.
- Each microservice is designed as an independent component with its own APIs.

2. **FaaS Function Development:**

- Developers identify specific functions within microservices that can benefit from serverless architecture.
- They develop and deploy these functions as serverless functions on the FaaS platform.

3. **API Gateway Integration:**

- The API Gateway is configured to manage incoming API requests and route them to the appropriate microservices or serverless functions.
- Requests are routed based on URL paths or request parameters.

4. **Function Triggers:**

- Microservices can trigger serverless functions when specific events or conditions occur.
- For example, a user registration microservice can trigger a notification function when a new user signs up.

5. **Scalability:**

- During periods of high traffic, the FaaS platform automatically scales out the execution of serverless functions to meet demand.
- Microservices remain scalable, too, based on containerization or other scaling mechanisms.

6. **Inter-Service Communication:**

- Microservices and serverless functions communicate with each other via APIs or asynchronous messaging.
- Data sharing and coordination occur as needed.

7. **Data Management:**

- Data is stored and retrieved from a shared database that microservices and functions can access.
- Data consistency and security are maintained.

Postconditions:

- The company successfully integrates FaaS within its microservices architecture, achieving scalability and cost-efficiency.
- The system effectively handles API requests, triggers serverless functions, and communicates between microservices and functions.

Alternative Flows:

- Function Composition: Serverless functions can be composed to create complex workflows or orchestration tasks.
- Third-Party Integrations: Functions can interact with external APIs and services to extend functionality.

Exception Flows:

- Function Failures: Error handling mechanisms are in place to log issues and potentially trigger retries or notifications.
- Service Outages: In case of FaaS platform outages, microservices may temporarily handle functions to maintain service availability.

Benefits:

- **Scalability:** Automatically scale microservices and functions to accommodate varying workloads.
- **Cost Efficiency:** Pay only for the compute resources used during function execution.

- ☁ **Modularity:** Encapsulate logic within independent microservices and serverless functions.
- ☁ **Agility:** Rapidly deploy and update functions without affecting the entire system.
- ☁ **Responsiveness:** Handle incoming API requests and events in real-time.

This use case demonstrates how Function as a Service (FaaS) can complement a microservices architecture, offering flexibility, scalability, and cost savings in the development and deployment of modular software services.

UC 1.15 USE CASE TITLE: AUTOMATION OF REPETITIVE TASKS WITH FAAS

Description:

This use case illustrates how a company leverages FaaS to automate repetitive and time-consuming tasks, increasing efficiency and reducing manual labor.

Actors:

- ☁ Administrators: Users responsible for identifying and implementing task automation using FaaS.
- ☁ FaaS Platform: The provider of the Function as a Service platform.
- ☁ Task Sources: Systems or data sources that generate repetitive tasks.

Preconditions:

- ☁ The company has access to a FaaS platform capable of running serverless functions.
- ☁ Repetitive tasks and their triggers have been identified.

Main Flow:

1. **Task Identification:**

- Administrators identify repetitive tasks within the organization that are suitable for automation.
- Tasks can include data processing, report generation, notifications, and more.

2. **Function Development:**

- Administrators or developers create serverless functions to automate identified tasks.
- Functions are designed to execute specific actions when triggered.

3. **Task Triggers:**

- Triggers for the automated tasks are defined based on specific events, schedules, or data conditions.
- Triggers can be time-based (e.g., daily reports) or event-based (e.g., data arrival).

4. **FaaS Deployment:**

- Serverless functions are deployed on the FaaS platform.
- Functions are configured to respond to the defined triggers.

5. **Task Automation:**

- When a trigger event occurs or a schedule is met, the associated serverless function is executed automatically.
- The function performs the task without manual intervention.

6. **Notification and Reporting:**

- After task completion, the FaaS function can send notifications, reports, or updates to relevant stakeholders.

7. **Logging and Monitoring:**

- The FaaS platform provides monitoring and logging capabilities to track the execution of functions and task automation.
- Logs and metrics are used for auditing and performance analysis.

Postconditions:

- The company successfully automates repetitive tasks, reducing manual effort and increasing efficiency.
- Task automation leads to improved accuracy and consistency.

Alternative Flows:

- Task Queues: Serverless functions can be used to process tasks from a queue, ensuring orderly execution.
- Dynamic Triggers: Triggers can be dynamic, responding to changes in data or external conditions.

Exception Flows:

- Function Failures: Error handling mechanisms are in place to log issues and potentially trigger retries or notifications.
- Task Source Issues: If the source of the task data or events experiences problems, the FaaS automation system may need to adapt or handle exceptions gracefully.

Benefits:

- **Efficiency:** Reduce manual effort and save time by automating repetitive tasks.
- **Consistency:** Ensure that tasks are performed consistently and without human errors.
- **Scalability:** Easily scale task automation to handle increased workloads.
- **Flexibility:** Adapt and modify automation logic as business needs change.
- **Cost Savings:** Reduce labor costs associated with manual task execution.

This use case demonstrates how Function as a Service (FaaS) can be applied to automate repetitive tasks within an organization, leading to increased efficiency, accuracy, and time savings for employees.

UC 1.16: USE CASE TITLE: IoT DATA PROCESSING AND ANALYSIS WITH FAAS

CLOUD EMPOWERMENT

Description:

This use case outlines how an organization utilizes Function as a Service (FaaS) to process and analyze data generated by Internet of Things (IoT) devices in real-time, gaining valuable insights and enabling immediate actions.

Actors:

- IoT Devices: Sensors, cameras, and other IoT devices that generate data.
- FaaS Platform: The provider of the Function as a Service platform.
- Data Analysts: Users responsible for designing and implementing data processing functions.
- Action Handlers: Components or systems that take actions based on analyzed IoT data.

Preconditions:

- The organization has implemented IoT devices that generate data streams.
- A FaaS platform is available for deploying serverless functions.

Main Flow:

1. **IoT Data Ingestion:**
- Data generated by IoT devices, such as sensor readings, images, or telemetry data, is ingested into the FaaS platform.
- Data can be sent in real-time or collected periodically.

2. **Function Development:**
- Data analysts design and develop serverless functions for processing and analyzing IoT data.
- Functions are created to extract relevant information, perform calculations, or detect anomalies.

3. **Data Transformation:**

- Serverless functions process the incoming IoT data streams.
- Data transformation includes cleaning, normalization, and feature extraction as needed.

4. **Real-time Analysis:**

- Functions analyze the IoT data in real-time to identify patterns, trends, or anomalies.
- Analysis can include statistical calculations, machine learning models, or rule-based systems.

5. **Alerting and Action Triggering:**

- When critical events or anomalies are detected, serverless functions trigger immediate actions or alerts.
- Actions may include sending notifications, adjusting device settings, or initiating maintenance requests.

6. **Data Storage and Archiving:**

- Processed IoT data can be stored in databases or data warehouses for historical analysis or compliance purposes.

Postconditions:

- The organization effectively utilizes FaaS for IoT data processing and real-time analysis, enabling immediate responses to critical events.
- Valuable insights are gained from the analyzed IoT data.

Alternative Flows:

- Integration: FaaS functions can integrate with external systems or APIs for data enrichment or additional actions.
- Batch Processing: Some IoT data may be processed in batch mode for in-depth historical analysis.

Exception Flows:

- Function Failures: Error-handling mechanisms are in place to log issues and potentially trigger retries or notifications.

- Data Source Issues: In case of data source disruptions or data quality issues, the FaaS system may need to adapt or handle exceptions gracefully.

Benefits:

- **Real-Time Insights:** Gain immediate insights from IoT data, enabling rapid decision-making.
- **Scalability:** Automatically scale data processing capacity based on data volume.
- **Cost Efficiency:** Pay only for the compute resources used during function execution.
- **Responsiveness:** Trigger immediate actions in response to critical IoT events.
- **Data Analysis:** Analyze IoT data for predictive maintenance, optimization, or monitoring.

This use case demonstrates how Function as a Service (FaaS) can be a valuable tool for processing and analyzing data generated by IoT devices in real-time, enabling organizations to make informed decisions and respond swiftly to critical events.

1.3. CLOUD DEPLOYMENT MODELS

The various ways in which cloud computing resources and services are made available to users and organizations are referred to as cloud deployment models. These models specify how cloud infrastructure is configured and shared. There are several popular cloud deployment models, which include:

Public Cloud: A third-party cloud service provider owns and operates cloud services and resources in a **public cloud** deployment. These services are made available to the general public or a large industry group, and they can be accessed via the internet. Many organizations find public cloud services to be cost-effective because they are scalable and pay-as-you-go. Amazon Web Services (AWS), Microsoft Azure, and Google Cloud Platform are examples of public cloud providers (GCP).

Private Cloud: A private cloud is one that is dedicated to a single organization, whether it is hosted on-premises or by a third-party provider. This deployment model gives you more control over your infrastructure and resources, making it ideal for organizations that have stringent security, compliance, or performance requirements. Enterprises and government agencies frequently use private clouds.

Hybrid Cloud: Hybrid cloud deployments combine public and private cloud components. Using a hybrid cloud model, businesses can share data and applications between on-premises infrastructure and public or private cloud resources. This method allows for flexibility and scalability while still maintaining some control over sensitive data or critical workloads. Hybrid cloud solutions frequently necessitate efficient management and integration of on-premises and cloud environments.

Multi-Cloud: A multi-cloud deployment involves an organization utilizing services and resources from multiple cloud providers. This approach can provide redundancy, avoid vendor lock-in, and leverage specialized services from multiple providers. Managing a multi-cloud environment can be difficult because it requires orchestrating services across multiple platforms.

Community Cloud: A community cloud is a group of organizations that share a common interest, such as regulatory requirements or industry standards. These organizations work together to create and operate a cloud infrastructure that meets their specific requirements while sharing costs and benefits.

Distributed Cloud: A relatively newer concept in which cloud services are distributed to various locations, including the network's edge. This model seeks to bring cloud computing closer to where data is generated or consumed, reducing latency and improving performance for real-time applications. Distributed cloud is an extension of traditional cloud models that provides a more decentralized approach.

CLOUD EMPOWERMENT

Edge Cloud: At the network edge, edge cloud deployments bring cloud computing resources closer to end-users or IoT devices. This reduces latency and bandwidth usage for applications that require quick response times, such as autonomous vehicles, IoT sensors, and augmented reality. The most appropriate cloud deployment model is determined by an organization's specific requirements, which include factors such as data security, compliance, scalability, and cost considerations. Many organizations use a combination of these deployment models to meet a variety of business requirements. Some of these deployment models are detailed below.

1. Public Cloud:

DESCRIPTION:

In a public cloud deployment, cloud services and infrastructure are owned and operated by a third-party cloud service provider and are made available to the general public over the internet. Multiple organizations and individuals share the same underlying infrastructure, but their data and applications remain logically isolated.

KEY CHARACTERISTICS:

- Shared Resources: Multiple tenants share the same hardware, storage, and network infrastructure.
- Cost-Efficiency: Cost-effective due to resource sharing and pay-as-you-go pricing.
- Scalability: Easy scalability to accommodate varying workloads.
- Example Providers: Amazon Web Services (AWS), Microsoft Azure, Google Cloud Platform (GCP).

Use Case Example:

Netflix: Netflix uses AWS for its streaming services. It leverages the public cloud's scalability to handle high traffic during peak times.

2. Private Cloud:

DESCRIPTION:

A private cloud is dedicated to a single organization. It can be hosted on-premises or by a third-party provider. The infrastructure and services are not shared with other organizations, offering greater control and security.

KEY CHARACTERISTICS:

- Dedicated Resources: Resources are exclusively used by one organization.
- Control: Greater control over security, compliance, and customization.
- Cost: Potentially higher initial costs due to dedicated infrastructure.
- Example Providers: VMware, OpenStack, IBM Cloud.

Use Case Example:

Banks: Financial institutions often deploy private clouds to meet stringent regulatory requirements for data security and privacy.

3. Hybrid Cloud:

DESCRIPTION:

Hybrid cloud combines elements of both public and private clouds. It allows data and applications to be shared between them. Organizations can move workloads between public and private environments as needed.

KEY CHARACTERISTICS:

- Flexibility: Offers flexibility to choose the best environment for each workload.
- Data Portability: Data and applications can be migrated between environments.
- Complexity: Requires management of both on-premises and cloud resources.
- Example Providers: AWS Outposts, Azure Hybrid, Google Anthos.

Use Case Example:

CLOUD EMPOWERMENT

Retailers: Retail companies might use a private cloud for sensitive customer data and a public cloud for e-commerce applications.

4. Multi-Cloud:

DESCRIPTION:

Multi-cloud involves using services from multiple cloud providers simultaneously. Organizations may select the best services from each provider based on specific requirements.

KEY CHARACTERISTICS:

- **Vendor Diversity:** Utilizes services from multiple cloud vendors.
- **Avoids Vendor Lock-In:** Reduces dependency on a single provider.
- **Complexity:** Requires managing different vendor interfaces and integration.
- **Example Providers:** AWS, Azure, GCP, IBM Cloud, Oracle Cloud.

Use Case Example:

- SaaS Companies: Software as a Service (SaaS) providers might use a combination of multiple cloud providers to ensure redundancy and availability of their services.

Each cloud deployment model offers unique advantages and challenges. Organizations often choose a deployment model based on factors such as data sensitivity, regulatory compliance, scalability requirements, and budget constraints. In practice, some organizations may even use a combination of these models to meet their diverse needs, resulting in a complex but highly adaptable cloud infrastructure.

Chapter 2
Cloud Infrastructure

2.1. DATA CENTERS AND SERVER FARMS

DATA CENTER ARCHITECTURE:

Data center architecture refers to the design and layout of a facility that houses and manages computing, networking, and storage resources. The primary goal of data center architecture is to ensure the efficient and reliable operation of these resources while maximizing scalability and minimizing downtime. Here are some key components and concepts within data center architecture:

- **Servers:** Data centers house a large number of servers, which can vary from physical servers to virtual machines (VMs). These servers run applications and services.
- **Networking Infrastructure:** Data centers have complex networking infrastructure, including switches, routers, and load balancers, to ensure connectivity between servers and external networks.
- **Storage Infrastructure:** Data centers typically have various storage solutions such as Storage Area Networks (SANs) and Network-Attached Storage (NAS) to store and manage data.
- **Power and Cooling:** Data centers require significant power for their equipment and cooling systems to maintain an optimal temperature. Redundant power sources and cooling systems are critical to prevent downtime.
- **Security Measures:** Data centers implement strict security measures to protect against physical and cyber threats. These can include biometric access controls, surveillance, firewalls, and intrusion detection systems.

CLOUD EMPOWERMENT

- **Scalability:** Data center architecture must be designed to scale easily. This can involve modular designs that allow for the addition of more servers or infrastructure components as needed.
- **Redundancy and High Availability:** To ensure uptime, data centers often employ redundancy at various levels, including power, networking, and server configurations. This minimizes the risk of service interruptions.

VIRTUALIZATION:

Virtualization is a technology that allows multiple virtual instances (virtual machines or VMs) to run on a single physical server or across a cluster of servers. Here are some key aspects of virtualization in data center architecture:

- **Server Virtualization:** This is the most common form of virtualization. It enables a single physical server to run multiple VMs, each of which can run its own operating system and applications. This optimizes resource utilization and simplifies server management.
- **Network Virtualization:** Network virtualization abstracts network resources, making it possible to create virtual networks that operate independently of the physical network infrastructure. This is valuable for isolating traffic and enhancing security.
- **Storage Virtualization:** Storage virtualization abstracts storage resources from the physical storage devices. It allows for easier management and provisioning of storage capacity.
- **Desktop Virtualization:** Desktop virtualization allows remote access to virtualized desktop environments, making it easier to manage and secure desktop computing for a large number of users.
- **Application Virtualization:** Application virtualization isolates applications from the underlying operating system, enabling

65

them to run in self-contained environments. This simplifies application management and can enhance compatibility.

- **Management and Orchestration:** Virtualization often includes management and orchestration tools to provision, monitor, and manage virtual resources efficiently.

Virtualization is a key component of modern data center architecture, as it offers flexibility, resource optimization, and the ability to quickly adapt to changing workloads and demands.

2.2. NETWORKING IN THE CLOUD

The networking that occurs in the cloud is an essential component of cloud computing. Proper networking guarantees that data is sent in a manner that is safe, effective, and dependable. The design of cloud architectures that are safe, scalable, and efficient must begin with the implementation of these networking components. It is essential to ensure that they are aligned with the specific networking and security requirements of your organization before beginning the process of configuring and managing them.

In the context of cloud networking, the following is an overview of Virtual Private Clouds (VPC), Content Delivery Networks (CDNs), and Network Security Groups (NSGs):

VIRTUAL PRIVATE CLOUD (VPC):

DEFINITION:

A Virtual Private Cloud, also known as a VPC, is a virtual network environment that is housed within the physical infrastructure of a public cloud provider such as Amazon Web Services, Microsoft Azure, or Google Cloud. It gives users the ability to create compartmentalized and private network spaces within a public cloud environment.

Use cases are provided below to demonstrate the applications of virtual private clouds.

CLOUD EMPOWERMENT

When these use cases are taken into consideration, a Virtual Private Cloud lays the groundwork for the creation of environments in the cloud that are secure, isolated, and interconnected, thereby meeting a variety of technical and business requirements. These environments can meet the needs of a wide range of organizations. Because of their versatility and configurability, virtual private clouds (VPCs) make it possible for businesses to design cloud architectures that are uniquely suited to meet the requirements of their operations.

KEY FEATURES:

- **Isolation:** VPCs provide network isolation, allowing you to create multiple private networks within the cloud environment.
- **IP Address Management:** You can define IP address ranges, subnets, and routing within a VPC.
- **Security Groups:** VPCs allow you to set up security groups or network access control lists (NACLs) to control inbound and outbound traffic.
- **Connectivity:** VPCs can be connected to on-premises data centers or other VPCs to create hybrid cloud architectures.

UC2.1: HOSTING APPLICATIONS SECURELY IN THE CLOUD

SCENARIO: Assume a company wants to migrate its web application to the cloud to benefit from scalability and cost-efficiency. They are concerned about security and want to ensure that their application is separate from other cloud resources.

VPC USE CASE:

- The company can create a VPC in their chosen cloud provider's environment (e.g., AWS, Azure, or Google Cloud).

- Within this VPC, they can define multiple subnets, separating their application's front-end and back-end components into different subnets for added security.
- Security Groups and Network ACLs can be configured within the VPC to control inbound and outbound traffic to and from the application's resources. For example, they can restrict access to the application's database server to only allow traffic from the application server.
- By configuring Route Tables and Internet Gateways, the company can control traffic flow and provide secure external access to their application while keeping other resources within the VPC isolated from the internet.

BENEFITS:

- The application is hosted in a secure, isolated environment.
- Network traffic can be controlled and monitored effectively.
- Scalability is maintained as needed, as the VPC can grow with the application's demands.

UC2.2: CREATING ISOLATED DEVELOPMENT AND TESTING ENVIRONMENTS

SCENARIO: An organization wants to create separate, isolated environments for development and testing to ensure that changes do not impact the production system.

VPC Use Case:

- Multiple VPCs can be created, one for development and one for testing, within the cloud provider's infrastructure.
- Each VPC can have its own subnets, security groups, and network ACLs.
- Development and testing teams can work independently within their respective VPCs without interfering with each other.

- Data and resources from the production VPC can be replicated or shared with the development and testing environments as needed.

Benefits:

- Isolation prevents changes or issues in development or testing from affecting the production environment.
- Teams can experiment and innovate within their isolated environments.
- Security can be maintained, and access controls can be tailored for each environment.

UC2.3: ENABLING SECURE COMMUNICATION BETWEEN ON-PREMISES INFRASTRUCTURE AND THE CLOUD:

SCENARIO: A company has an on-premises data center with critical resources and wants to extend its infrastructure to the cloud while maintaining secure communication.

VPC USE CASE:

- The company can establish a Virtual Private Network (VPN) connection or use Direct Connect (for AWS) or ExpressRoute (for Azure) to create a secure connection between their on-premises network and the cloud VPC.
- Within the VPC, they can create a VPN Gateway or Virtual Interface to facilitate this connection.
- Security measures such as encryption and tunneling can be implemented to ensure data traveling between the on-premises network and the cloud VPC remains secure.
- Network routing configurations can be set up to direct traffic between on-premises and cloud resources.

BENEFITS:

- Secure and private communication is established between on-premises and cloud environments.
- Resources in the cloud can be seamlessly integrated into existing infrastructure.
- Data can be transferred securely, making it suitable for sensitive workloads.

CONTENT DELIVERY NETWORKS (CDNS):

DEFINITION:

A Content Delivery Network, also known as a CDN, is a network of distributed servers that are geographically dispersed all over the world. The purpose of content delivery networks, or CDNs, is to provide users with web content and other resources, such as images and videos, in a prompt and effective manner. Use cases and examples are provided below to demonstrate the capabilities of content delivery networks (CDNs) to improve the performance, scalability, and security of web-based services and content delivery, thereby making CDNs an indispensable resource for businesses that operate in the digital landscape.

KEY FEATURES:

- **Caching:** CDNs cache content at edge locations, reducing the load on origin servers and improving content delivery speed.
- **Load Balancing:** CDNs often include load balancing capabilities to distribute incoming traffic across multiple servers or locations.
- **Distributed Architecture:** CDNs have multiple edge servers in various geographic locations to reduce latency for end-users.

UC 2.4: SPEEDING UP WEBSITE AND WEB APPLICATION PERFORMANCE:

CLOUD EMPOWERMENT

SCENARIO: Take, for example, an online retail company that runs a website and caters to clients all over the world. They want to make sure that the user experience they provide is quick and responsive, regardless of where the user is located geographically.

CDN USE CASE:

- The e-commerce company subscribes to a CDN service and configures it to cache their website's static content (e.g., images, JavaScript, CSS files) on the CDN's distributed servers, often referred to as "edge servers" or "PoPs" (Points of Presence).
- When a user requests a page from the website, the CDN automatically serves the static content from the nearest edge server, reducing latency and load times.
- Dynamic content, such as user-specific data, is fetched from the origin server as usual but benefits from the reduced load on the origin server due to the CDN's caching of static assets.
- The CDN also optimizes content delivery through techniques like TCP optimization, route optimization, and connection multiplexing, further enhancing performance.

BENEFITS:

- Faster load times, which improve user experience and reduce bounce rates.
- Reduced load on the origin server, saving bandwidth and server resources.
- Improved scalability, as the CDN handles traffic spikes and surges.

UC 2.5: DELIVERING HIGH-QUALITY VIDEO STREAMING:

Scenario: A media streaming company wants to deliver high-quality video content to users globally, including viewers on various devices like smartphones, tablets, and smart TVs.

CDN USE CASE:

- The media streaming company utilizes a CDN optimized for video streaming.
- Video content is encoded into different quality levels (bitrates and resolutions) and stored on the CDN's edge servers.
- When a user requests a video, the CDN detects the user's device and network conditions and delivers the appropriate quality level, ensuring smooth playback without buffering.
- Adaptive streaming technologies like Dynamic Adaptive Streaming over HTTP (DASH) or HTTP Live Streaming (HLS) are often used to switch between quality levels in real-time as network conditions change.
- The CDN's edge servers also employ content prefetching to reduce start-up delays.

BENEFITS:

- High-quality video playback without buffering, even on slower connections.
- Global scalability and reduced server load due to CDN distribution.
- Improved user engagement and retention.

UC2.6: DDoS Attack Mitigation by Distributing Traffic Across Multiple Locations

Scenario: A well-known online service is frequently the focus of Distributed Denial of Service, or DDoS, attacks, which are launched in an effort to flood the targeted company's servers and make the service unavailable.

CLOUD EMPOWERMENT

CDN USE CASE:

- The online service leverages a CDN with DDoS protection capabilities.
- When a DDoS attack is detected, the CDN can distribute incoming traffic across its geographically dispersed edge servers.
- Traffic is scrubbed and filtered at the edge servers to identify and block malicious traffic, preventing it from reaching the origin server.
- The CDN absorbs the excess traffic and absorbs the brunt of the attack, mitigating the impact on the service's infrastructure.
- In some cases, CDN providers also offer Web Application Firewall (WAF) services to protect against application layer attacks.

BENEFITS:

- DDoS attack traffic is absorbed and mitigated at the network edge.
- Service availability is maintained, and the origin server is shielded from attack traffic.
- Enhanced security and protection against various attack vectors.

NETWORK SECURITY GROUPS (NSGS):

DEFINITION:

Network Security Groups (NSGs) are security rules and policies used to control inbound and outbound network traffic in a Virtual Network (VNet) or VPC. In these use cases, Network Security Groups (NSGs) play a vital role in enforcing security policies, isolating resources, and protecting virtual machines and applications from unauthorized access, ultimately enhancing the security posture of organizations in the cloud.

KEY FEATURES:

- **Firewall Rules:** NSGs allow you to define rules that permit or deny traffic based on source and destination IP addresses, ports, and protocols.
- **Layered Security:** NSGs can be applied at both the subnet and individual resource levels, providing layered security controls.
- **Logging and Monitoring:** Some cloud providers offer logging and monitoring features to track network traffic and security events.

UC2.7: ENFORCING NETWORK SECURITY POLICIES BY CONTROLLING TRAFFIC FLOWS

Scenario: Imagine a company that hosts critical web applications in the cloud and wants to enforce strict security policies to protect against unauthorized access and potential threats.

NSG USE CASE:

The company sets up new network security groups (NSGs) and connects those NSGs to their Azure Virtual Network or AWS Virtual Private Cloud. These NSGs have security rules that specify what kinds of traffic are allowed and what kinds are not.

They configure inbound and outbound rules within the NSGs to control the flow of traffic. For example,

- they may allow incoming HTTP and HTTPS traffic while denying all other incoming connections.
- NSGs can be associated with specific subnets, network interfaces, or individual VMs, allowing granular control over traffic flows.
- By specifying source and destination IP ranges, ports, and protocols in NSG rules, the company enforces security policies that restrict access to only authorized parties.

BENEFITS:

- Enhanced security by controlling and monitoring network traffic.

- Reduced attack surface by permitting only necessary traffic.
- Granular control over network communication within the virtual network.

UC 2.8: SEGMENTING NETWORK TRAFFIC TO RESTRICT ACCESS TO SENSITIVE RESOURCES:

Scenario: A cloud environment is being used by a financial institution to host sensitive customer data as well as financial application software. They have a responsibility to ensure that this information is segregated and that only authorized personnel can access it.

NSG USE CASE:

- The institution creates multiple NSGs and associates them with different subnets within their VPC or Virtual Network.
- NSGs associated with the sensitive data subnet contain strict security rules that permit traffic only from authorized IP addresses (e.g., the institution's offices).
- Subnets containing fewer sensitive resources have less restrictive NSG rules, allowing broader access as needed.
- By segmenting the network in this way, the institution ensures that sensitive data is isolated and protected while other parts of the network can operate with more flexibility.

BENEFITS:

- Strong segregation of sensitive data from other resources.
- Enhanced compliance with data privacy regulations.
- Restrictive security controls for critical areas of the network.

UC 2.9: PROTECTING VIRTUAL MACHINES (VMs) AND APPLICATIONS FROM UNAUTHORIZED ACCESS:

Scenario: In order to successfully run its online store, an e-commerce company utilizes a number of virtual machines (VMs) hosted in the cloud. They have a responsibility to make sure that these virtual machines are protected from intrusion by unauthorized users.

NSG USE CASE:

- The company associates NSGs with each VM or group of VMs.
- They define security rules within the NSGs to allow only essential traffic. For example, they permit incoming traffic on port 80 (HTTP) and port 443 (HTTPS) to their web servers but block all other incoming traffic.
- Rules for outbound traffic can also be configured to control what the VMs can connect to outside the network.
- By consistently applying NSGs to all VMs, the company maintains a uniform security posture across its infrastructure.

Benefits:

- Protection of VMs and applications from unauthorized access.
- Reduced attack surface and exposure to security threats.
- Consistent and manageable security policies across VMs.

2.3. STORAGE IN THE CLOUD

Cloud storage is a service that allows you to store and access data, such as files, documents, photos, and videos, on remote servers over the internet rather than on your local computer or hardware. Cloud storage is also known as internet-based storage or online storage. Typically, cloud service providers will maintain this data in the data centers that they own and operate.

The use of cloud storage provides a number of benefits, including the following:

Accessibility: You are able to access your data from any location provided you have a connection to the internet. This makes it simple to work with other people, and it also enables you to access your files from a variety of devices.

Scalability: Ability of most cloud storage services to allow you to easily expand or reduce the amount of storage space you have available based on your requirements. Maintaining your own hardware might be more expensive in the long run than renting cloud storage where you only pay for the space you take up.

Backup and Recovery: Cloud storage solutions typically include backup and data recovery features, which can assist in preventing the loss of your files in the event that the underlying hardware fails, the data is stolen, or other unforeseen circumstances occur.

Security: Reputable cloud storage providers protect your data from unauthorized access by implementing security measures such as encryption and access controls.

Collaboration: Many cloud storage services offer collaboration features that make it easier to work with other people on documents and projects. These features include file sharing, real-time editing, and version control.

The following are examples of popular cloud storage providers:

- **Google Drive** is a free cloud storage service that integrates with Google Workspace (previously known as G Suite) for file sharing and collaboration.
- **Dropbox** is well-known for its intuitive interface as well as its capability to synchronize files.
- **OneDrive** by Microsoft is a cloud storage service that is integrated with Microsoft 365 (previously known as Office 365) and provides seamless integration with Windows.
- The **iCloud** service offered by Apple allows users' data to be synchronized across all of their Apple-branded devices.

- The **Amazon Web Services** (AWS) S3 service provides businesses and developers with an alternative that is more technically advanced for storing large amounts of data.
- **Box** focuses on providing businesses with a secure platform for file sharing and collaboration.

When selecting a service for cloud storage, it is important to take into consideration a number of different aspects, such as the storage capacity, pricing, level of security, and level of integration with the tools and devices that you already use. It is absolutely necessary for you to read through the terms of service and privacy policies of the provider in order to gain an understanding of how your data will be handled and protected by the provider. There are primarily three categories of cloud storage, such as object storage. Stacking in blocks Keeping track of files. In order to satisfy the wide variety of storage needs their organizations have in the cloud, many businesses actually employ a combination of these various storage technologies.

These are analyzed further below with the help of a case study to demonstrate their qualities and advantages.

1. OBJECT STORAGE:

Definition:
Object storage is a storage technology that stores data as objects. Each object consists of the data, metadata, and a unique identifier. It is highly scalable, making it suitable for storing vast amounts of unstructured data, such as images, videos, backups, and documents.

KEY CHARACTERISTICS:

- **Scalability:** Object storage can handle massive datasets and is designed to scale horizontally, making it ideal for cloud-scale applications.
- **Metadata:** Each object includes metadata that provides information about the object, such as creation date, content type, and permissions.

- **Durability:** Object storage systems are highly durable, with data often replicated across multiple data centers or regions for redundancy.

Example: Amazon S3 (Simple Storage Service) is a popular object storage service. You can store files as objects in S3 buckets. For instance, a media company can use S3 to store videos, images, and other media files. Each file is treated as an object with its metadata.

2. BLOCK STORAGE

Definition:

Block storage divides data into blocks, each with its address. It resembles traditional hard drives and is suitable for structured data that requires high performance and low latency, such as databases and virtual machines.

KEY CHARACTERISTICS:

- **Performance:** Block storage offers high-performance I/O and is often used for applications that require fast and consistent access to data.
- **Data Integrity:** It provides data integrity features like checksums and redundancy to ensure that data remains intact.
- **Flexibility:** Users can format block storage devices with their chosen file system and install operating systems and applications on them.

Example: Amazon Elastic Block Store (EBS) in AWS is an example of block storage. Users can create EBS volumes, attach them to EC2 instances, and use them as storage for databases, file systems, or applications.

3. FILE STORAGE

DEFINITION:

File storage is a storage technology that organizes data into a hierarchical file structure. It is suitable for shared access and collaboration on files and directories and is commonly used for user home directories, shared network drives, and application data.

KEY CHARACTERISTICS:

- **File System:** File storage systems provide a file system interface, allowing multiple users or applications to access and modify files concurrently.

- **Access Control:** They offer access control mechanisms, including file-level permissions and user authentication, to manage file access.

- **Ease of Use:** File storage is user-friendly and often used for storing documents, media files, and application data that requires shared access.

Example: Amazon Elastic File System (EFS) is an example of file storage. It allows you to create and manage file systems that can be mounted on multiple EC2 instances. For instance, EFS is suitable for shared application data, web content, and user home directories.

Comparison and Use Cases:

Object Storage: Best suited for storing unstructured data at scale, such as media files, backups, and archives.

Block Storage: Ideal for applications that require high-performance, low-latency access to structured data, like databases and virtual machines.

File Storage: Suitable for shared access and collaboration on files and directories, often used for user home directories, application data, and shared network drives.

2.4. COMPUTE RESOURCES

"Compute resources" in the context of cloud computing refer to the computing power and resources made available to users by cloud service providers. These resources are essential for carrying out various computing tasks in the cloud, including processing data and running applications. The following are some essential elements of cloud computing resources:

Virtual Machines (VMs): In the cloud, virtual machines are a fundamental type of compute resource. Users of the cloud can create and manage virtual machines (VMs) to run applications and services because they are merely virtualized versions of physical servers. Users can choose the best resources for their needs by configuring CPU, memory, and storage in VMs in a variety of ways.

Containers: Containers offer a compact and effective method for deploying applications and all of their dependencies. Although they run in separate environments, they share the kernel of the host operating system. Containerized applications can be managed and scaled with the aid of container orchestration platforms like Kubernetes.

Serverless computing: By abstracting away the underlying infrastructure, serverless computing enables developers to concentrate solely on writing code without having to manage servers. Based on the workload of the application, cloud providers automatically allot and scale compute resources as necessary.

Some cloud service providers offer bare metal instances, which give users direct access to hardware resources without the use of virtualization. These instances are appropriate for workloads needing specialized hardware configurations or high performance.

CPU, Memory, and Storage: When using the cloud, users frequently have the option of customizing the CPU, RAM, and storage resources for their virtual machines or containers. As the demands of their workload change, they can scale these resources up or down.

Tensor Processing Units (TPUs) and **Graphics Processing Units (GPUs)** are two types of specialized hardware accelerators that can be used in the cloud. They are especially helpful for high-performance parallel processing tasks like machine learning, scientific simulations, and rendering.

Load balancers: To guarantee availability and even resource utilization, load balancers distribute incoming network traffic among various instances of an application.

Auto Scaling: Based on traffic or workload patterns, cloud providers offer auto scaling services that automatically adjust the number of compute resources. This improves resource usage and upholds application performance.

Function-as-a-Service (FaaS): Platforms that provide code execution in response to events, like AWS Lambda or Azure Functions, enable developers to respond to events without having to set up or maintain servers. These procedures automatically scale and use compute resources as necessary.

Elasticity: The capacity to swiftly and automatically scale up or down compute resources in response to variations in demand. This guarantees that applications can effectively handle a range of workloads.

Network Resources: Since cloud applications must communicate with one another and with outside services, network resources are closely related to compute resources. To manage network-related aspects of compute resources, cloud providers offer a variety of networking features like virtual networks, subnets, and security groups.

Cloud computing is a flexible and economical solution for a variety of applications and workloads because cloud users typically pay for the compute resources they use, frequently on a pay-as-you-go or subscription basis. Here we discuss in detail about Virtual Machines (VMs), Containers and Kubernetes, and, Serverless Computing. In practice, the choice between these compute resources depends on factors like application architecture, resource requirements, development approach, and operational preferences. Many organizations leverage a combination of these technologies to optimize their cloud-based workloads.

1. VIRTUAL MACHINES (VMS)

DEFINITION:

Virtual Machines are virtualized versions of physical computers. They allow you to run multiple operating systems and applications on a single physical host server. VMs are a fundamental compute resource in cloud computing, offering flexibility and isolation.

KEY CHARACTERISTICS:

- **Isolation:** Each VM operates independently, with its own dedicated resources and operating system.
- **Scalability:** VMs can be easily scaled up or down to meet changing workloads.
- **Compatibility:** VMs can run a wide range of operating systems and applications.

Example: Amazon EC2 (Elastic Compute Cloud) is a popular VM service in AWS. Users can create VM instances, known as EC2 instances, and choose from a variety of pre-configured virtual machine types. For instance, an e-commerce company can use EC2 instances to host its web application, database, and analytics workloads, each within its own VM for isolation and scalability.

2. CONTAINERS AND KUBERNETES:

DEFINITION:

Containers are lightweight, standalone executable packages that include everything needed to run an application, including code, runtime, libraries, and dependencies. **Kubernetes** is an orchestration platform that automates the deployment, scaling, and management of containerized applications.

KEY CHARACTERISTICS:

- **Portability:** Containers can run consistently across different environments, from development to production.
- **Efficiency:** Containers share the host OS kernel, making them more efficient than VMs in terms of resource utilization.
- **Scaling:** Kubernetes provides automated scaling based on resource usage and user-defined policies.

Example: Docker is a popular containerization platform. An e-commerce company can package its web application, including all dependencies, into a Docker container. **Kubernetes,** when used in conjunction with a container orchestration service like Google Kubernetes Engine (GKE) or Amazon EKS, can manage the deployment, scaling, and high availability of these containers, ensuring the web application is always available and responsive.

3. SERVERLESS COMPUTING:

DEFINITION:

Serverless computing, also known as **Function-as-a-Service (FaaS)**, allows developers to execute code in response to events without managing servers. It abstracts server management, enabling developers to focus solely on writing code.

KEY CHARACTERISTICS:

- Event-Driven: Serverless functions are triggered by events, such as HTTP requests, database changes, or file uploads.
- Auto-scaling: Cloud providers automatically scale serverless functions based on demand.
- Pay-as-You-Go: You are charged only for the compute resources used during function execution.

Example: AWS Lambda is a well-known serverless computing service. Consider a ride-sharing app that calculates ride fares. Instead of running a continuously running server, the app can use AWS Lambda. When a ride is completed, an event triggers a Lambda function to calculate the fare, and it scales automatically to handle the volume of ride requests without managing server instances.

Comparison and Use Cases:

Virtual Machines (VMs): Best suited for running complex applications that require dedicated resources and isolation, as well as compatibility with specific operating systems.

Containers and Kubernetes: Ideal for packaging, deploying, and managing microservices-based applications with high portability and scalability requirements.

Serverless Computing: Well-suited for event-driven, short-duration tasks and services that require automatic scaling and cost-efficiency without managing servers.

Chapter 3
Cloud Providers

Companies known as cloud service providers (CSPs) provide people, businesses, and organizations with a range of cloud computing services and resources. These services, which can include computing power, storage, databases, networking, analytics, machine learning, and more, are typically provided online. The top cloud service providers are listed below.

Amazon Web Services (AWS): AWS is one of the largest and most widely used cloud service providers in the world. It offers a vast array of services, including computing, storage, machine learning, and Internet of Things (IoT), among others.

Microsoft Azure: Microsoft's cloud platform, Azure, provides a wide range of services for building, deploying, and managing applications. It's known for its integration with Microsoft's software products like Windows Server and Office 365.

Google Cloud Platform (GCP): GCP offers cloud computing, storage, machine learning, and data analytics services. It's known for its strengths in data and analytics, as well as its machine learning capabilities.

IBM Cloud: IBM Cloud provides infrastructure as a service (IaaS), platform as a service (PaaS), and software as a service (SaaS) solution. It also offers AI and blockchain services.

Oracle Cloud: Oracle Cloud offers cloud infrastructure and a wide range of cloud services, including database, application, and platform services. It's known for its strong presence in the enterprise database market.

Alibaba Cloud: Alibaba Cloud is a leading cloud provider in Asia and offers a broad set of cloud services, including computing, data storage, and artificial intelligence. It's known for its global data center presence.

Salesforce: Salesforce is a cloud-based customer relationship management (CRM) platform. It also offers various cloud services and applications for sales, marketing, and customer service.

Adobe Creative Cloud: Adobe's Creative Cloud is a subscription-based service that provides access to a suite of creative software tools and services, including Photoshop, Illustrator, and Premiere Pro.

Tencent Cloud: Tencent Cloud is a Chinese cloud provider that offers a range of cloud services, including computing, data storage, and artificial intelligence, with a focus on the Asia-Pacific region.

Rackspace Technology: Rackspace provides managed cloud services, including cloud infrastructure management, security, and application services. It partners with multiple cloud providers, including AWS, Azure, and GCP.

DigitalOcean: DigitalOcean specializes in providing cloud infrastructure and services for developers. It's known for its simplicity and developer-friendly tools.

These cloud service providers compete on a number of different fronts, such as the range and depth of services they offer, pricing, performance, security, and the presence of international data centers. When choosing a provider to host their applications and data in the cloud, businesses frequently base their decision on their unique needs and specifications. Recall that the cloud computing environment is dynamic, with providers frequently enhancing their offerings. When choosing cloud providers, it's crucial to stay current on the newest products and trends in the sector.

3.1. AMAZON WEB SERVICES (AWS)

CORE SERVICES AND OFFERINGS

Amazon Web Services (AWS) is a comprehensive cloud computing platform provided by Amazon.com. AWS offers a wide range of services and solutions that cater to various computing needs, from basic infrastructure services to advanced machine learning capabilities. Here, we'll explore some of the core AWS services and their possible examples and applications:

1. AMAZON EC2 (ELASTIC COMPUTE CLOUD):

Description: EC2 provides scalable, resizable virtual machines (VMs) or instances in the cloud. Users can choose from a variety of instance types to meet their specific workload requirements.

Examples and Applications:

Web Hosting: Host websites and web applications on EC2 instances. For example, an e-commerce site can run on multiple EC2 instances for high availability.

Data Processing: Use EC2 instances to process large datasets, run simulations, or perform scientific computations.

Machine Learning: Train machine learning models on EC2 instances with powerful GPUs.

2. AMAZON S3 (SIMPLE STORAGE SERVICE):

Description: S3 is a scalable object storage service designed for storing and retrieving data. It offers high durability and availability.

Examples and Applications:

Data Backup: Store backups of critical data and files. For instance, an enterprise can back up its databases and user data to S3.

Static Website Hosting: Host static websites by serving HTML, CSS, and JavaScript files directly from S3.

Big Data: Use S3 to store large datasets for data analytics and processing using services like AWS Glue and Amazon Athena.

3. AWS LAMBDA:

Description: Lambda is a serverless compute service that allows users to run code in response to events. Users are charged based on the compute time used.

Examples and Applications:

Event-Driven Functions: Automatically resize images upon upload, process data from IoT devices, or trigger notifications in response to events.

CLOUD EMPOWERMENT

Microservices: Develop and run individual functions for various parts of a larger application architecture.

Scheduled Tasks: Execute code on a schedule, such as data cleanup or report generation.

4. AMAZON RDS (RELATIONAL DATABASE SERVICE):

Description: RDS offers managed relational database services for popular database engines like MySQL, PostgreSQL, and Microsoft SQL Server.

Examples and Applications:

E-commerce: Use RDS to store product information, customer data, and transaction records for an online store.

Content Management: Manage content and user data for a content management system (CMS) or blog platform.

Enterprise Applications: Run mission-critical applications with reliable and scalable databases.

5. AMAZON VPC (VIRTUAL PRIVATE CLOUD):

Description: VPC enables users to create isolated networks within the AWS cloud, providing control over network configurations, security, and connectivity.

Examples and Applications:

Secure Application Hosting: Host applications in a private network with controlled access via VPN or Direct Connect.

Multi-Tier Architectures: Build multi-tier applications with public-facing web servers and private database servers.

Hybrid Cloud: Connect on-premises data centers to AWS using VPC for a hybrid cloud setup.

6. AMAZON SNS (SIMPLE NOTIFICATION SERVICE) AND SQS (SIMPLE QUEUE SERVICE):

Description: SNS allows for the sending of messages to distributed systems, while SQS is a fully managed message queuing service for decoupling and scaling microservices.

Examples and Applications:

Event-Driven Architectures: Use SNS to notify other services about events (e.g., user registration) and SQS to handle background processing.

Decoupling Components: Implement a message-based architecture to separate components in a scalable manner.

Mobile App Notifications: Send push notifications to mobile app users through SNS.

These are just a few of the numerous services that AWS provides. Over 200 services, including those for compute, storage, databases, analytics, machine learning, security, and more, are part of AWS' extensive ecosystem. AWS is used by businesses to create scalable, dependable, and affordable solutions across a variety of sectors and use cases.

3.2. MICROSOFT AZURE

CORE SERVICES AND OFFERINGS

Microsoft Azure is a cloud computing platform and infrastructure offered by Microsoft. It provides a wide range of cloud services that cater to various computing needs, from infrastructure and platform services to advanced AI and machine learning capabilities. Let's explore some of the core Azure services and their possible examples and applications:

1. AZURE VIRTUAL MACHINES (VMS):

Description: Azure VMs provide scalable and resizable virtual machines in the cloud. Users can choose from a variety of pre-configured images or create custom VMs to meet specific workload requirements.

Examples and Applications:

CLOUD EMPOWERMENT

Web Applications: Host web applications and websites on Azure VMs. For example, an e-commerce site can run on multiple VMs for scalability.

Development and Testing: Quickly provision VMs for development and testing environments, saving time and resources.

High-Performance Computing: Use Azure VMs with GPU support for tasks like rendering, simulations, and machine learning.

2. AZURE BLOB STORAGE:

Description: Azure Blob Storage is a scalable and cost-effective object storage service designed for storing and managing unstructured data, such as documents, images, and videos.

Examples and Applications:

Data Backup: Store backups of critical data and files in Blob Storage. For instance, an organization can back up its databases and user data.

Media and Content Delivery: Serve media files, videos, and large documents directly from Blob Storage.

Data Analytics: Store and analyze large datasets for data analytics and processing using services like Azure Databricks and Azure Data Lake Storage.

3. AZURE FUNCTIONS:

Description: Azure Functions is a serverless compute service that allows users to run code in response to events. Users are charged based on the number of executions and execution time.

Examples and Applications:

Event-Driven Applications: Automatically trigger code execution in response to events like file uploads, database changes, or IoT sensor readings.

Microservices: Develop and run individual functions as microservices, simplifying application architecture and scalability.

Scheduled Tasks: Execute code on a schedule, such as data processing, report generation, or cleanup tasks.

4. AZURE SQL DATABASE:

Description: Azure SQL Database is a fully managed relational database service that supports popular database engines like SQL Server.

Examples and Applications:

Line-of-Business Applications: Store and manage data for business-critical applications, such as CRM or ERP systems.

Web Applications: Host data-driven web applications with scalability and high availability.

Analytics and Reporting: Use Azure SQL Database as a data source for analytics and reporting tools.

5. AZURE VIRTUAL NETWORK (VNET):

Description: Azure Virtual Network enables users to create isolated networks within the Azure cloud, providing control over network configurations, security, and connectivity.

Examples and Applications:

Secure Application Hosting: Host applications in a private network with controlled access via VPN or ExpressRoute.

Multi-Tier Architectures: Build multi-tier applications with public-facing web servers and private database servers.

Hybrid Cloud: Connect on-premises data centers to Azure using VNet for a hybrid cloud setup.

6. AZURE SERVICE BUS AND AZURE EVENT GRID:

Description: Azure Service Bus is a messaging service for reliable message queuing and communication, while Azure Event Grid is an event routing service for event-driven architectures.

Examples and Applications:

Event-Driven Architectures: Use Azure Service Bus for messaging between services, and Azure Event Grid for routing and reacting to events.

Decoupling Components: Implement a message-based architecture to separate components and scale independently.

IoT and Serverless: Collect and process data from IoT devices or trigger serverless functions based on events.

These are just a few of the numerous services that Azure provides. Over 200 services across compute, storage, databases, analytics, AI, machine learning, security, and more are part of Azure's extensive ecosystem. Businesses use Azure to create intelligent, scalable solutions for a range of industries and use cases.

3.3. GOOGLE CLOUD PLATFORM (GCP)

CORE SERVICES AND OFFERINGS

Google Cloud Platform (GCP) is a comprehensive cloud computing platform offered by Google. It provides a wide range of cloud services and solutions to address various computing needs, from infrastructure and data analytics to machine learning and AI capabilities. Let's explore some of the core GCP services and their possible examples and applications:

1. GOOGLE COMPUTE ENGINE:

Description: Compute Engine offers scalable and customizable virtual machines (VMs) in the cloud. Users can choose from various pre-configured machine types or create custom VMs.

Examples and Applications:

Web Applications: Host web applications and websites on Compute Engine VMs. For example, a news website can run on multiple VMs for high availability.

Big Data Processing: Deploy VMs for data processing, analytics, and machine learning tasks, leveraging GCP's data services.

High-Performance Computing: Use Compute Engine instances with GPUs for scientific simulations, rendering, and deep learning.

2. GOOGLE CLOUD STORAGE:

Description: Google Cloud Storage is an object storage service designed for storing and managing unstructured data, including images, videos, backups, and documents.

Examples and Applications:

Data Backup: Store backups of critical data and files in Google Cloud Storage. For instance, an organization can back up its databases and user data.

Content Delivery: Serve media files, videos, and large documents directly from Cloud Storage, enhancing content delivery performance.

Data Analytics: Store and analyze large datasets for data analytics and processing using GCP's data analytics services.

3. GOOGLE CLOUD FUNCTIONS:

Description: Google Cloud Functions is a serverless compute service that allows users to run code in response to events. Users are billed based on the number of executions and execution time.

Examples and Applications:

Event-Driven Applications: Trigger code execution in response to events like file uploads, database changes, or IoT sensor data.

Microservices: Develop and deploy individual functions as microservices, simplifying application architecture.

Scheduled Tasks: Execute code on a schedule, such as data processing, report generation, or cleanup tasks.

4. GOOGLE CLOUD SQL:

Description: Google Cloud SQL is a fully managed relational database service that supports popular database engines like MySQL, PostgreSQL, and SQL Server.

Examples and Applications:

Line-of-Business Applications: Store and manage data for business-critical applications, such as financial systems or CRM.

Web Applications: Host data-driven web applications with automatic failover and scalability.

Analytics and Reporting: Use Cloud SQL as a data source for analytics and reporting tools.

5. GOOGLE VIRTUAL PRIVATE CLOUD (VPC):

Description: Google VPC enables users to create isolated networks within the GCP cloud, providing control over network configurations, security, and connectivity.

Examples and Applications:

Secure Application Hosting: Host applications in a private network with controlled access via VPN or Dedicated Interconnect.

Multi-Tier Architectures: Build multi-tier applications with public-facing web servers and private database servers.

Hybrid Cloud: Connect on-premises data centers to GCP using VPC for a hybrid cloud setup.

6. GOOGLE CLOUD PUB/SUB AND CLOUD FUNCTIONS:

Description: Cloud Pub/Sub is a messaging service for event-driven architectures, and Cloud Functions allows you to run code in response to Pub/Sub events.

Examples and Applications:

Event-Driven Architectures: Use Cloud Pub/Sub for asynchronous messaging between services, and trigger Cloud Functions to react to events.

Decoupling Components: Implement a message-based architecture to separate components and scale independently.

IoT and Real-Time Data: Collect and process data from IoT devices or handle real-time data streams with Pub/Sub and Cloud Functions.

These are only a few of the numerous services that GCP provides. Over 200 services across compute, storage, databases, analytics, AI, machine learning, security, and more are included in the vast ecosystem of GCP. Businesses use GCP to develop adaptable, knowledgeable, and data-driven solutions for numerous sectors and use cases.

3.4. OTHER CLOUD PROVIDERS

There are several other cloud providers besides the major players like AWS, Azure, and GCP as mentioned above. Let's explore some of them and their core services along with possible examples and applications:

1. IBM CLOUD:

Description: IBM Cloud offers a range of cloud services and solutions that cater to enterprises, emphasizing hybrid and multi-cloud capabilities. IBM Cloud provides services for compute, storage, databases, AI, and more.

Core Services and Offerings:

IBM Virtual Servers: Similar to VMs on other cloud platforms, users can deploy and manage virtual servers to run applications and workloads.

IBM Cloud Object Storage: Scalable object storage for storing and managing unstructured data.

IBM Db2 on Cloud: A fully managed database service for deploying and managing Db2 databases.

IBM Watson: Access to IBM's AI and machine learning capabilities for natural language processing, image recognition, and more.

Examples and Applications:

Hybrid Cloud: Enterprises can use IBM Cloud to extend their on-premises infrastructure to the cloud seamlessly.

AI-Powered Applications: Develop applications that leverage IBM Watson for chatbots, sentiment analysis, and predictive analytics.

Data Analytics: Utilize IBM Cloud for data warehousing, big data analytics, and data science projects.

2. ORACLE CLOUD:

Description: Oracle Cloud is Oracle Corporation's cloud computing platform, providing a suite of cloud services, including infrastructure, databases, applications, and developer tools.

Core Services and Offerings:

CLOUD EMPOWERMENT

Oracle Cloud Infrastructure (OCI): A set of computes, storage, and networking services, including VMs, block storage, and load balancing.

Oracle Autonomous Database: A self-driving, self-repairing, and self-securing database service.

Oracle Cloud Applications: Enterprise-grade SaaS solutions for areas like ERP, HCM, and CRM.

Oracle Cloud Functions: Serverless compute service for running code in response to events.

Examples and Applications:

Enterprise Workloads: Run business-critical applications and databases on Oracle Cloud.

Autonomous Databases: Simplify database management with Oracle's autonomous database service.

SaaS Integration: Extend and integrate Oracle Cloud Applications with custom solutions.

3. ALIBABA CLOUD:

Description: Alibaba Cloud, also known as Alibaba Cloud Computing, is the cloud computing arm of Alibaba Group. It is one of the largest cloud providers in China and offers a comprehensive suite of cloud services.

Core Services and Offerings:

Elastic Compute Service (ECS): Scalable compute instances similar to VMs.

Object Storage Service (OSS): Scalable and highly available object storage.

Alibaba Cloud Database Services: A range of database solutions including Apsara DB for RDS and NoSQL databases.

Alibaba Cloud Machine Learning: Access to AI and machine learning tools and algorithms.

Examples and Applications:

Global Expansion: Businesses can use Alibaba Cloud to expand their presence in Asia and around the world.

E-commerce and Retail: Alibaba Cloud supports the e-commerce and retail sector with various solutions, including big data analytics.

IoT and Edge Computing: Utilize Alibaba Cloud for IoT projects and edge computing applications.

4. DIGITALOCEAN:

Description: DigitalOcean is a cloud provider known for its simplicity and developer-friendly approach. It offers cloud computing solutions primarily targeted at developers, startups, and small to medium-sized businesses.

Core Services and Offerings:

Droplets: Virtual private servers (similar to VMs) for running applications and websites.

Kubernetes: Managed Kubernetes clusters for container orchestration.

App Platform: A Platform-as-a-Service (PaaS) solution for building, deploying, and scaling web applications.

Examples and Applications:

Developer-Focused Projects: DigitalOcean is popular among developers for hosting web applications, blogs, and personal projects.

Startup Acceleration: Many startups use DigitalOcean for its ease of use and cost-effectiveness.

Containerized Applications: Deploy containerized applications using DigitalOcean Kubernetes.

These cloud service providers provide distinctive services and are appropriate for a range of use cases and industries. These providers are chosen by organizations based on things like particular workload requirements, geographic locations, and strategic preferences.

Chapter 4
Cloud Management and Orchestration

4.1. CLOUD MANAGEMENT TOOLS

Effectively managing and optimizing cloud computing resources and services requires both cloud management and orchestration.

1. MANAGEMENT OF CLOUDS:

To control, monitor, and optimize their use of cloud resources and services, organizations use a set of practices, instruments, and policies collectively referred to as cloud management. It entails a variety of duties and tasks aimed at guaranteeing that cloud environments are effective, secure, economical, and in line with an organization's business objectives. Cloud management's essential elements include:

Creating and configuring cloud resources like virtual machines, databases, and storage, frequently with the aid of automation tools.

Monitoring and Performance Management: Constantly keeping an eye on the functionality and efficiency of cloud-based resources, programs, and services. For the purpose of quickly identifying and resolving issues, metrics and logs must be collected.

Implementing security controls and compliance guidelines to safeguard cloud-based resources and data. This covers encryption, compliance audits, and identity and access management.

Cost optimization: Controlling cloud expenses by keeping an eye on resource usage, putting cost controls in place, and optimizing resource allocation in accordance with actual requirements.

Scaling and Elasticity: Dynamically modifying the number of resources (using auto-scaling, for example) to correspond to shifts in workload demand, ensuring that applications function effectively under a range of circumstances.

The management of a resource's entire lifecycle, from creation and scaling to decommissioning and disposal, is known as resource lifecycle management.

Implementing backup and disaster recovery techniques will protect data and guarantee business continuity.

Establishing and enforcing policies for resource provisioning, access control, and resource naming conventions are all parts of governance and policy management.

Monitoring and managing cloud services to adhere to SLAs and guarantee high availability and dependability.

CLOUD ORCHESTRATION

The automated coordination and management of numerous cloud resources, services, and workflows in order to accomplish a particular business objective or application deployment is known as cloud orchestration. It entails creating and implementing workflows for efficiently provisioning, configuring, and managing cloud resources. Cloud orchestration's essential features include:

Determining the order of tasks and actions necessary to deploy and manage cloud resources is known as a workflow. This may include the sequence in which resources are created, configured, and integrated.

Automation: Using orchestration tools and scripts, automating the execution of workflows. Consistency is ensured while manual intervention is reduced.

Integration is the process of creating end-to-end workflows by integrating various cloud services, APIs, and tools. For instance, this could entail tying infrastructure provisioning and application deployment together.

CLOUD EMPOWERMENT

Scalability and Flexibility: Coordinating resources to scale up or down in response to demand, enabling applications to change their operations to accommodate shifting workloads.

Monitoring and error handling: Constantly keeping an eye out for errors, exceptions, and performance problems in orchestration workflows. putting in place mechanisms for error handling and recovery.

Self-Service Portals: By providing self-service portals or interfaces, users can use predefined orchestration workflows to request and manage cloud resources and services.

Managing resources across various cloud providers and on-premises environments, multi-cloud orchestration enables businesses to take advantage of hybrid and multi-cloud strategies.

Automating and orchestrating complicated cloud deployments requires the use of orchestration platforms and tools like **Kubernetes, Apache Airflow, Terraform**, and tools specific to each cloud provider. In situations where applications and services require complex, multi-step workflows or span multiple cloud providers, cloud orchestration is especially useful. It supports businesses in managing their cloud infrastructure and services more efficiently, effectively, and with less manual labor.

1. AWS MANAGEMENT CONSOLE:

DESCRIPTION:

The AWS Management Console is a web-based interface provided by Amazon Web Services (AWS) for managing and monitoring AWS resources and services. It offers a user-friendly, graphical way to interact with AWS.

KEY FEATURES:

- **Service Management:** Users can create, configure, and manage a wide range of AWS services, such as EC2 instances, S3 buckets, RDS databases, Lambda functions, and more.
- **Resource Monitoring:** The console provides dashboards and monitoring tools to track resource usage, health, and performance.
- **Access Control:** AWS Identity and Access Management (IAM) allows users to control access and permissions for AWS resources.
- **Billing and Cost Management:** Users can view and analyze their AWS billing and cost data to optimize spending.

Examples:

EC2 Instance Launch: An IT administrator can use the AWS Management Console to launch new EC2 instances with specific configurations, such as instance type, operating system, and security groups.

UC 4.1: USE CASE TITLE: EC2 INSTANCE LAUNCH

SCENARIO:

As an IT administrator, it is your job to provision new virtual servers (EC2 instances) on Amazon Web Services to support different applications. You can launch brand-new EC2 instances with particular configurations catered to the requirements of your company using the AWS Management Console.

Steps:

1. Log in to AWS Management Console:

- Open a web browser and navigate to the AWS Management Console.
- Sign in using your AWS account credentials.

2. Access EC2 Dashboard:

CLOUD EMPOWERMENT

After logging in, you'll be presented with the AWS Management Console dashboard. To access the EC2 service, click on "Services" in the top left corner, then select "EC2" under the "Compute" section.

3.   Launch an EC2 Instance:

In the EC2 Dashboard, click the "Instances" link on the left-hand navigation pane.

Click the "Launch Instance" button to initiate the EC2 instance creation process.

4.   Choose an Amazon Machine Image (AMI):

In the "Choose an Amazon Machine Image (AMI)" step, you select the operating system and software stack for your EC2 instance. For example, you can choose an Amazon Linux AMI for a general-purpose server.

5.   Choose an Instance Type:

In the "Choose an Instance Type" step, you select the instance type based on your workload requirements. AWS provides a variety of instance types with varying CPU, memory, and GPU capabilities. For instance, you can choose a compute-optimized instance for CPU-intensive tasks.

6.   Configure Instance Details:

In the "Configure Instance Details" step, you can set additional options such as the number of instances to launch, network settings, IAM role assignments, and user data scripts.

7.   Add Storage:

In the "Add Storage" step, you configure the storage volumes for your EC2 instance. You can specify the size and type of the root volume and add additional data volumes as needed.

8.   Configure Security Group:

In the "Configure Security Group" step, you define the inbound and outbound traffic rules for the EC2 instance. For example, you can open ports 22 (SSH) and 80 (HTTP) to allow SSH and web traffic.

9.   Review and Launch:

☁ Review the configuration details to ensure they are correct. You can make changes by navigating back to previous steps if needed.

10.   Launch the Instance:

☁ Click the "Launch" button to initiate the EC2 instance creation process.

11.   Create or Use an Existing Key Pair:

☁ If you don't have an existing key pair for SSH access, create a new one. Download the private key and securely store it.

12.   Launch Instances:

☁ Click the "Launch Instances" button. AWS will now start provisioning the EC2 instance based on your specifications.

Example Use Case Outcome:

In this use case, you've successfully used the AWS Management Console to launch an EC2 instance. This instance can now be used to host applications, run workloads, or perform specific tasks within your AWS environment. You can repeat these steps to launch additional EC2 instances with varying configurations, scale your infrastructure as needed, and manage instances efficiently using AWS Cloud Management Tools.

UC 4.2: USE CASE TITLE - S3 BUCKET MANAGEMENT

SCENARIO:

To securely store and share datasets, a data analyst can create and manage S3 buckets.

Consider yourself a data analyst who is in charge of safely managing, storing, and distributing datasets on AWS. To facilitate data storage and collaboration, you will create and manage S3 buckets using the AWS Management Console.

STEPS:

1.   Log in to AWS Management Console:

☁ Open a web browser and navigate to the AWS Management Console.

☁ Sign in with your AWS account credentials.

2. Access S3 Dashboard:

☁ After logging in, you'll be presented with the AWS Management Console dashboard. To access the S3 service, click on "Services" in the top left corner, then select "S3" under the "Storage" section.

3. Create a New S3 Bucket:

☁ In the S3 Dashboard, click the "Create bucket" button.

☁ Enter a unique and descriptive name for your bucket. Bucket names must be globally unique across all of AWS.

☁ Select the AWS region in which you want to create the bucket. Choose a region that aligns with your data locality requirements.

☁ Click "Create."

4. Configure Bucket Properties:

☁ After creating the bucket, you can configure various properties such as versioning, logging, and event notifications. For example, you can enable versioning to track changes to objects in the bucket.

5. Set Bucket Permissions:

☁ In the "Permissions" tab, you can define access control for the bucket. You can create and configure Access Control Lists (ACLs) or use Bucket Policies. For instance, you can grant read-only access to specific IAM users or roles.

6. Add Objects to the Bucket:

☁ Navigate to the bucket you created and click the "Upload" button to add objects (files) to the bucket. You can upload files individually or in bulk.

7. Set Object Permissions:

☁ You can configure permissions for individual objects within the bucket. For example, you can make specific files public for download while keeping others private.

8. Enable Logging (Optional):

☁ If necessary, you can enable server access logging for the bucket to track requests made to objects.

9. Configure Event Notifications (Optional):

☁ If needed, set up event notifications to trigger actions when objects are created, deleted, or modified in the bucket.

10. Review and Manage Bucket Content:

☁ You can use the S3 Dashboard to manage the contents of your bucket, including renaming, deleting, and organizing objects into folders.

Example Use Case Outcome:

In this use case, you created an S3 bucket and successfully managed its properties, permissions, and contents using the AWS Management Console. Datasets can now be shared and stored securely in this S3 bucket with the proper access controls. The S3 bucket serves as a focal point for data management and team collaboration in your AWS environment because it allows data analysts and other team members to work together by uploading, downloading, and analyzing data.

UC4.3: USE CASE TITLE: LAMBDA FUNCTION DEPLOYMENT

SCENARIO:

Developers can utilize the console to deploy an AWS Lambda serverless function and configure triggers like S3 events or API Gateway endpoints. Consider yourself a developer tasked with deploying a serverless function using AWS Lambda. The AWS Management Console must be used to create, configure, and set up the triggers for the Lambda function, including S3 uploads and API Gateway requests.

STEPS:

1. Log in to AWS Management Console:

☁ Open a web browser and navigate to the AWS Management Console.

☁ Sign in with your AWS account credentials.

2. Access Lambda Dashboard:

☁ After logging in, you'll be presented with the AWS Management Console dashboard. To access the Lambda service, click on "Services" in the top left corner, then select "Lambda" under the "Compute" section.

3.   Create a New Lambda Function:

☁ In the Lambda Dashboard, click the "Create function" button.

☁ Choose the "Author from scratch" option to create a custom Lambda function.

4.   Configure Function Details:

☁ In the "Configure function" step, provide details for your Lambda function:

☁ Function name: Enter a unique and descriptive name for your function.

☁ Runtime: Choose the programming language runtime for your function (e.g., Python, Node.js, Java).

☁ Execution role: Create a new role or choose an existing IAM role that grants necessary permissions to your function.

5.   Write or Upload Code:

☁ In the "Function code" section, you can write your Lambda function code directly in the editor or upload a deployment package, which includes your code and any dependencies.

6.   Configure Triggers:

☁ In the "Add triggers" section, you can set up triggers for your Lambda function. For example:

☁ S3 Bucket: To trigger the Lambda function whenever a new object is uploaded to an S3 bucket, select "S3" and choose the bucket and event type (e.g., "ObjectCreated").

☁ API Gateway: To create a RESTful API with AWS API Gateway as a trigger, select "API Gateway" and configure your API endpoints.

7.   Configure Function Settings (Optional):

- You can set advanced configurations such as memory allocation, timeout, and environment variables based on your function's requirements.

8.   Review and Create:

- Review the configuration details to ensure they are correct.
- Click the "Create function" button to deploy your Lambda function.

EXAMPLE USE CASE OUTCOME:

You created and configured a Lambda function using the AWS Management Console successfully in this use case. Now, events like fresh S3 uploads or API Gateway requests can automatically trigger this Lambda function. For instance, the Lambda function can automatically resize a new image when it is uploaded to an S3 bucket or carry out other processing operations. This shows the strength and adaptability of serverless computing with AWS Lambda as well as the simplicity of management with AWS Cloud Management Tools.

2. AZURE PORTAL:

DESCRIPTION:

The Azure Portal is the web-based management interface provided by Microsoft Azure. It offers a centralized hub for managing Azure resources and services, making it easy for users to build, deploy, and manage applications.

KEY FEATURES:

- **Resource Creation:** Users can provision and configure various Azure resources, including VMs, databases, web apps, and AI services.
- **Monitoring and Diagnostics:** Azure Monitor provides insights into the health and performance of resources, with customizable dashboards and alerting.

CLOUD EMPOWERMENT

- **Identity and Access Management:** Azure Active Directory (Azure AD) integration allows users to manage identity and access control for Azure services.
- **Cost Management:** Azure Cost Management helps users track and optimize cloud spending.

UC 4.4: USE CASE TITLE: VIRTUAL MACHINE DEPLOYMENT

SCENARIO:

A cloud engineer can use the Azure Portal to create and customize virtual machines, including selecting an OS, specifying resource sizes, and configuring networking. Imagine you are a cloud engineer responsible for deploying virtual machines on Azure to support various workloads. Using the Azure Portal, you will create and customize virtual machines, including selecting an operating system, specifying resource sizes, and configuring networking.

STEPS:

1. Log in to Azure Portal:
   - Open a web browser and navigate to the Azure Portal.
   - Sign in using your Azure account credentials.
2. Access Virtual Machines (VMs) Dashboard:
   - After logging in, you'll be on the Azure Portal dashboard. To access the Virtual Machines service, click on "Virtual machines" under the "All services" section on the left-hand navigation pane.
3. Create a New Virtual Machine:
   - In the Virtual Machines dashboard, click the "Add" button to create a new VM.
4. Configure Basics:

- In the "Basics" tab of the VM creation wizard, provide the following details:
- Project Details: Select the Azure subscription and resource group for your VM.
- Instance Details: Enter a unique name for your VM.
- Region: Choose the Azure region where you want to deploy the VM.
- Image: Select the base operating system image for your VM. You can choose from various Windows and Linux distributions.
- Authentication Type: Choose how you want to authenticate to the VM (e.g., SSH public key, password).
- Username and Password/SSH Key: Provide the necessary authentication credentials.

5. Configure Disks:
   - In the "Disks" tab, configure the disk options for your VM, including OS disk type, data disks, and disk size.

6. Configure Networking:
   - In the "Networking" tab, set up the networking options for your VM:
   - Virtual Network: Select an existing virtual network or create a new one.
   - Subnet: Specify the subnet within the virtual network.
   - Public IP: Choose whether to assign a public IP address to the VM.
   - Network Security Group (NSG): Configure network security rules for inbound and outbound traffic.

7. Configure Management and Advanced:
   - In the "Management" tab, you can configure features like boot diagnostics, guest OS settings, and extensions.
   - In the "Advanced" tab, you can set up features like auto-shutdown, backup, and monitoring.

8. Review + Create:

CLOUD EMPOWERMENT

- Review the configuration details to ensure they are correct.
- Click the "Review + create" button to validate your settings.

9. Create the Virtual Machine:
- After validation, click the "Create" button to deploy the virtual machine.

USE CASE OUTCOME:

You've successfully created and customized a virtual machine using the Azure Portal in this use case. Within your Azure environment, you can now use this VM to host applications, run workloads, or carry out particular tasks. Azure is a powerful platform for managing and deploying infrastructure because it provides additional options for scaling, managing, and monitoring virtual machines (VMs) in accordance with your unique requirements.

UC 4.5: USE CASE TITLE: APP SERVICE CREATION

SCENARIO:

Using Azure App Service, a developer can create and deploy a web application as well as control its scaling and deployment slots. Consider yourself a developer in charge of designing and launching a web application on Azure. You will create and set up an Azure App Service to host your web application using the Azure Portal. Additionally, you'll organize deployment slots for testing and staging as well as manage the application's scaling.

Steps:

1. Log in to Azure Portal:
- Open a web browser and navigate to the Azure Portal.
- Sign in using your Azure account credentials.

2. Access App Services Dashboard:

☁ After logging in, you'll be on the Azure Portal dashboard. To access the App Services, click on "App Services" under the "All services" section on the left-hand navigation pane.

3. Create a New App Service:

    ☁ In the App Services dashboard, click the "Add" button to create a new App Service.

4. Configure Basics:

    ☁ In the "Basics" tab of the App Service creation wizard, provide the following details:

    ☁ Project Details: Select the Azure subscription and resource group for your App Service.

    ☁ Instance Details: Enter a unique name for your App Service.

    ☁ Publish: Choose how you want to deploy your application. For example, you can select "Code" for source code deployment or "Docker Container" for containerized applications.

    ☁ Operating System: Select the desired operating system for your web app.

    ☁ Region: Choose the Azure region where you want to deploy the App Service.

    ☁ App Service Plan: Create a new plan or choose an existing one. The plan defines the resources and scaling options for your web app.

    ☁ Configure Monitoring and Security (Optional):

    ☁ In the "Monitoring" tab, you can set up application insights and diagnostics for your web app.

    ☁ In the "Identity" tab, configure identity settings if required.

5. Review + Create:

    ☁ Review the configuration details to ensure they are correct.

    ☁ Click the "Review + create" button to validate your settings.

6. Create the App Service:

    ☁ After validation, click the "Create" button to deploy the App Service.

CLOUD EMPOWERMENT

USE CASE OUTCOME:

In this use case, you created and deployed an Azure App Service to host your web application using the Azure Portal. Your web application is currently operational and obtainable on Azure. By changing the App Service Plan settings, you can control how your application scales based on demand. Additionally, you can create deployment slots (such as staging and testing) to make it easier to test and stage new web application versions before deploying them to a live environment. Azure App Service is a strong hosting platform for web applications because it has a variety of features for continuous deployment, scaling, and monitoring.

UC4.6: USE CASE TITLE: AZURE FUNCTION CONFIGURATION

Scenario:

A DevOps engineer can set up triggers, configure Azure Functions, and keep track of function executions through the portal.

Imagine that you are an Azure Functions configuration and management engineer. Your objective is to design, set up, and keep track of Azure Functions that carry out particular tasks when prompted by various events. You will configure triggers and keep an eye on how these operations are carried out using the Azure Portal.

Steps:

1. Log in to Azure Portal:
   - Open a web browser and navigate to the Azure Portal.
   - Sign in using your Azure account credentials.
2. Access Azure Functions Dashboard:
   - After logging in, you'll be on the Azure Portal dashboard. To access Azure Functions, click on "Function Apps" under the "All services" section on the left-hand navigation pane.
3. Create a New Function App:

- ☁ In the Azure Functions dashboard, click the "Add" button to create a new Function App.
- ☁ Provide the necessary details for the Function App, including subscription, resource group, name, and hosting plan (consumption or dedicated).

4. Create a New Function:

- ☁ Once the Function App is created, navigate to it and click the "Functions" section.
- ☁ Click the "+ Add" button to create a new function.
- ☁ Choose a development environment (e.g., JavaScript, C#, Python) and select a trigger for your function. Triggers can include HTTP, Blob storage, Azure Service Bus, and more.

5. Configure Function Settings:

- ☁ In the function configuration, you can set up parameters and bindings, define input and output data, and write the code for your function. For example, if you selected an HTTP trigger, you can configure the route and method for your HTTP endpoint.

6. Test the Function:

- ☁ Use the built-in testing capabilities within the Azure Portal to test your function. You can provide sample input data and see the function's output.

7. Set Up Triggers:

- ☁ After creating the function, you can set up triggers to define when and how the function should execute. For example, you can configure a timer trigger to run the function on a schedule or set up a blob trigger to execute the function when a new file is uploaded to Azure Blob Storage.

8. Monitor Function Executions:

- ☁ Azure provides monitoring and logging capabilities to track the execution of your functions. You can view execution history, logs, and performance metrics through the Azure Portal. This helps in troubleshooting and performance optimization.

Use Case Outcome:

You created, configured, and monitored Azure Functions using the Azure Portal successfully in this use case. Now that various triggers and events, such as HTTP requests or file uploads, have occurred, these functions are prepared to react. The Azure Portal offers a user-friendly interface for effectively managing and monitoring these functions, and Azure Functions offers a scalable and serverless compute platform for running code in response to events.

3. GOOGLE CLOUD CONSOLE

DESCRIPTION:

The Google Cloud Console is Google Cloud's web-based interface for managing and interacting with Google Cloud Platform (GCP) services. It provides tools for creating, configuring, and monitoring GCP resources.

KEY FEATURES:

- **Resource Management:** Users can create and manage a wide range of GCP resources, including Compute Engine instances, Cloud Storage buckets, BigQuery datasets, and more.
- **Monitoring and Logging:** Google Cloud Monitoring and Google Cloud Logging allow users to monitor and troubleshoot resource performance and track application logs.
- **Identity and Access Management:** Google Identity and Access Management (IAM) provides fine-grained access control over GCP resources.
- **Billing and Cost Management:** Users can view billing reports, set budgets, and manage costs within the console.

UC 4.7: USE CASE TITLE: COMPUTE ENGINE INSTANCE CREATION

SCENARIO:

A system administrator can create virtual machines (VMs) with specific CPU, memory, and image type configurations using the Google Cloud Console.

Think of yourself as a system administrator tasked with building virtual machines (VMs) on Google Cloud to accommodate various workloads. You can create and modify Compute Engine instances using the Google Cloud Console by specifying settings for the CPU, memory, and image type.

STEPS:

1. Log in to Google Cloud Console:
   - Open a web browser and navigate to the Google Cloud Console.
   - Sign in with your Google Cloud account credentials.
2. Access Compute Engine Dashboard:
   - After logging in, you'll be on the Google Cloud Console dashboard. To access Compute Engine, click on "Compute Engine" under the "Compute" section in the left-hand navigation pane.
3. Create a New Compute Engine Instance:
   - In the Compute Engine dashboard, click the "Create" button to create a new Compute Engine instance.
4. Configure Instance Details:
   - In the "Create an instance" form, provide the following details:
   - Name: Enter a unique name for your instance.
   - Region and Zone: Choose the Google Cloud region and zone where you want to deploy the instance.
   - Machine Type: Select the CPU and memory configuration for your VM. You can choose predefined machine types or

customize the instance with custom CPU and memory allocations.

5. Choose Boot Disk:

    - In the "Boot disk" section, select the image type and size for the boot disk. You can choose from various operating system images or use a custom image.

    - Configure Additional Options (Optional):

    - You can configure optional settings such as adding GPUs, enabling Cloud Identity-Aware Proxy, and configuring metadata or startup scripts.

6. Set Up Networking:

    - Configure the network settings for your instance. You can choose an existing VPC (Virtual Private Cloud) network or create a new one. Specify the external IP address and firewall rules as needed.

    - Add SSH Keys (Optional):

    - If you want to SSH into the instance, you can add SSH keys for authentication.

7. Review and Create:

    - Review the configuration details to ensure they are correct.

    - Click the "Create" button to create the Compute Engine instance.

8. Monitor and Manage:

    - Once the instance is created, you can monitor its status, view performance metrics, and manage it through the Google Cloud Console. You can also SSH into the instance directly from the Console.

USE CASE OUTCOME:

In this use case, you've successfully used the Google Cloud Console to create and customize a Compute Engine instance. This VM can now be used to host applications, run workloads, or perform specific tasks within your Google Cloud environment. Google Cloud offers additional features for scaling, managing, and monitoring instances based on your specific requirements, making it a powerful platform for virtual machine deployment and management.

UC 4.8: USE CASE TITLE: CLOUD STORAGE MANAGEMENT

SCENARIO:

A data engineer can create buckets for Cloud Storage, upload data, and set up access controls for sharing data.

Consider yourself a data engineer in charge of overseeing and archiving data in Google Cloud Storage. To securely share data with others, you must create Cloud Storage buckets, upload data to them, and set up access control. To carry out these actions, you will make use of the Google Cloud Console.

STEPS:

1.   Log in to Google Cloud Console:
    - Open a web browser and navigate to the Google Cloud Console.
    - Sign in with your Google Cloud account credentials.
2.   Access Cloud Storage Dashboard:
    - After logging in, you'll be on the Google Cloud Console dashboard. To access Cloud Storage, click on "Storage" under the "Storage" section in the left-hand navigation pane.
3.   Create a New Cloud Storage Bucket:
    - In the Cloud Storage dashboard, click the "Create bucket" button to create a new Cloud Storage bucket.
    - Enter a unique and descriptive name for your bucket.
    - Choose the Google Cloud project associated with the bucket.

- Select the location where you want to store the data. You can choose a regional or multi-regional location based on your needs.

4. Configure Bucket Permissions:
    - After creating the bucket, you can configure access control settings:
    - Access Control List (ACL): You can set ACLs to define who has access to the bucket and what level of access they have (e.g., read, write, delete).
    - Identity and Access Management (IAM): Use IAM policies to define fine-grained permissions for users, groups, and service accounts. For example, you can grant a specific user read-only access to the bucket.

5. Upload Data to the Bucket:
    - Navigate to the bucket you created and click the "Upload files" button to upload data to the bucket.
    - You can upload individual files or entire folders. Specify the data you want to upload from your local machine.

6. Configure Object Lifecycle (Optional):
    - If necessary, you can configure object lifecycle policies to automatically delete or transition objects to other storage classes based on criteria like age or access frequency.

7. Generate Signed URLs (Optional):
    - If you need to share data securely with external parties, you can generate signed URLs that grant temporary, time-limited access to specific objects within the bucket.

8. View and Manage Data:
    - Use the Google Cloud Console to view, manage, and organize data within the bucket. You can create folders, rename objects, and delete data as needed.

USE CASE OUTCOME:

In this use case, you've successfully used the Google Cloud Console to create a Cloud Storage bucket, upload data, and configure access control settings. Your data is securely stored in Cloud Storage, and you can easily manage, share, and organize it through the console. Google Cloud Storage offers reliable and scalable object storage for various data storage and retrieval needs, and Cloud Management Tools simplify the process of managing and securing your data in the cloud.

UC 4.9: USE CASE TITLE: BIG QUERY DATASET CONFIGURATION

SCENARIO:

To analyze large datasets, a data scientist can set up datasets in BigQuery, make tables, and run SQL queries. Consider yourself a data scientist who has been given the assignment to set up datasets in Google BigQuery for extensive dataset analysis. To extract insights from your data, you must create datasets, define tables, and execute SQL queries. To carry out these actions, you will make use of the Google Cloud Console.

STEPS:

1. Log in to Google Cloud Console:
   - Open a web browser and navigate to the Google Cloud Console.
   - Sign in with your Google Cloud account credentials.
2. Access BigQuery Dashboard:
   - After logging in, you'll be on the Google Cloud Console dashboard. To access BigQuery, click on "BigQuery" under the "Big Data" section in the left-hand navigation pane.
3. Create a New Dataset:
   - In the BigQuery dashboard, select your project or create a new one.
   - Right-click on the project and choose "Create dataset."
   - Enter a unique and descriptive name for your dataset.

CLOUD EMPOWERMENT

- Set the default table expiration if needed.
- Configure dataset location and encryption settings.
- Click the "Create dataset" button.

4. Create Tables within the Dataset:
   - After creating the dataset, you can create tables within it to store your data.
   - Click on the dataset's name, then click the "Create table" button.
   - Choose the table's creation method (e.g., manually, from a source).
   - Configure the table's schema, specifying column names and data types.
   - Define other table properties like partitioning, clustering, and time-based settings as needed.
   - Click the "Create table" button.

5. Import Data into Tables:
   - To analyze data, you need to import it into the tables you've created.
   - Click on the table's name, then click the "Create table" button.
   - Choose the data source (e.g., Google Cloud Storage, a local file, another table).
   - Configure data import options such as format, schema auto-detection, and source details.
   - Click the "Create table" button to import the data.

6. Run SQL Queries:
   - Use the Query Editor in the BigQuery dashboard to write and execute SQL queries on your data.
   - Write queries to retrieve, analyze, and transform the data within your dataset.
   - You can save and share query results as well.

7. Schedule Queries (Optional):

- For recurring analysis tasks, you can schedule queries to run at specific intervals.
- Define query parameters and scheduling settings to automate data processing.
- Monitor and Visualize Results:
- Utilize the query history and monitoring tools in BigQuery to track query performance and optimize as needed.
- You can also use Data Studio or other visualization tools to create reports and dashboards based on your query results.

Use Case Outcome:

You have successfully configured datasets in BigQuery, created tables, imported data, and executed SQL queries to analyze large datasets using the Google Cloud Console in this use case. Now that BigQuery has powerful analytical capabilities, you can explore, transform, and learn from your data. Data scientists can effectively analyze large datasets in the cloud with Google BigQuery's scalable and fully managed data warehouse.

The administration and monitoring of cloud resources and services are made much easier thanks to these cloud management consoles. They enable users to effectively manage their cloud infrastructure and applications, whether they are developers, administrators, or data analysts.

4.2. INFRASTRUCTURE AS CODE (IAC)

Infrastructure as Code (IaC) is a fundamental concept in cloud computing and DevOps that allows you to manage and provision infrastructure using code rather than manual processes. This approach provides several benefits, including repeatability, version control, and the ability to automate infrastructure provisioning and configuration. Three popular tools for implementing IaC are Terraform, AWS

CLOUD EMPOWERMENT

CloudFormation, and Azure Resource Manager Templates. Let's explore each of these tools in detail:

TERRAFORM

DESCRIPTION:

Terraform is an open-source infrastructure as code tool created by HashiCorp. It is designed to provision and manage infrastructure across various cloud providers, on-premises environments, and even third-party services.

KEY FEATURES:

- **Declarative Syntax:** Terraform uses a declarative language to define infrastructure as code. You specify the desired state of your infrastructure, and Terraform determines the actions needed to achieve that state.
- **Provider Agnostic:** Terraform supports multiple cloud providers (e.g., AWS, Azure, Google Cloud), making it a versatile choice for multi-cloud or hybrid cloud environments.
- **Resource Management:** Infrastructure components are defined as "resources" in Terraform, and you can create, update, or destroy them as needed.
- **Dependency Management:** Terraform manages resource dependencies automatically, ensuring that resources are provisioned in the correct order.

UC 4.10: USE OF TERRAFORM TO DEFINE AND PROVISION AN AWS

Virtual Private Cloud (VPC), including subnets, security groups, and routing tables, all as code. Here's an example of Terraform code to create an AWS EC2 instance:

```hcl
resource "aws_instance" "example" {
  ami           = "ami-0c55b159cbfafe1f0"
  instance_type = "t2.micro"
}
```

AWS CLOUDFORMATION:

DESCRIPTION:

AWS CloudFormation is a native service provided by Amazon Web Services (AWS) for defining and provisioning AWS infrastructure as code. It uses JSON or YAML templates to declare the resources and their dependencies.

KEY FEATURES:

- **AWS Integration:** CloudFormation seamlessly integrates with AWS services, making it well-suited for AWS-focused environments.
- **Stack Management:** You create "stacks" in CloudFormation, which represent a collection of AWS resources that can be managed as a single unit.
- **Change Sets:** Before applying changes to your infrastructure, CloudFormation allows you to preview changes via change sets, ensuring safety.
- **Rollback and Rollback Triggers:** CloudFormation can automatically roll back changes in case of failures, and you can define rollback triggers for custom actions.

UC 4.11: USE OF AWS CLOUD FORMATION

You can use AWS CloudFormation to define and provision an entire web application stack, including EC2 instances, RDS databases, and S3 buckets. Here's a simplified YAML template example:

CLOUD EMPOWERMENT

```yaml
Resources:
  MyInstance:
    Type: AWS::EC2::Instance
    Properties:
      InstanceType: t2.micro
      ImageId: ami-0c55b159cbfafe1f0
```

AZURE RESOURCE MANAGER TEMPLATES:

DESCRIPTION:

Azure Resource Manager (ARM) Templates are used to define and provision Azure infrastructure as code. These templates use JSON or Bicep (a domain-specific language) to declare Azure resources and their configurations.

KEY FEATURES:

Azure Integration: ARM templates are tightly integrated with Microsoft Azure, making them the primary choice for Azure-centric environments.

- **Resource Groups:** Resources are grouped into "resource groups," and you can manage and deploy resources within these groups collectively.
- **Validation and Deployment:** ARM templates are validated for syntax and schema correctness before deployment. Azure also provides template parameterization for flexibility.
- **Linked Templates:** You can use linked templates to modularize and reuse parts of your infrastructure code.

UC 4.12: USE OF ARM TEMPLATE

125

You can use ARM templates to define and provision an Azure Virtual Network with subnets, network security groups, and virtual machines. Here's an example snippet:

In the below command prompt, read as:
$schema""https://schema.management.azure.com/schemas/2019-04-01/deploymentTemplate.json#",

```json
{
  "$schema": "https://schema.management.azure.com/schemas/2019-(
  "contentVersion": "1.0.0.0",
  "resources": [
    {
      "type": "Microsoft.Network/virtualNetworks",
      "name": "MyVNet",
      "location": "[resourceGroup().location]",
      "properties": {
        "addressSpace": {
          "addressPrefixes": [
            "10.0.0.0/16"
          ]
        }
      }
    }
  ]
}
```

In multi-cloud or cloud-specific environments, Terraform, AWS CloudFormation, and Azure Resource Manager Templates are effective tools for managing infrastructure as code. Your specific preferences and needs for your cloud provider will determine which of these tools you choose.

CLOUD EMPOWERMENT

4.3. ORCHESTRATION AND AUTOMATION

Orchestration and automation play a crucial role in cloud technology, enabling the efficient execution of tasks, workflows, and processes. AWS Lambda, Azure Logic Apps, and Google Cloud Functions are powerful tools for orchestrating and automating workflows and processes in the cloud. They enable you to build efficient, event-driven systems that respond to various events and triggers, making cloud automation scalable and accessible to developers and operations teams.

Three cloud services that excel in this domain are AWS Lambda, Azure Logic Apps, and Google Cloud Functions. Let's delve into each of them with detailed examples.

1. AWS LAMBDA

DESCRIPTION:

AWS Lambda is a serverless compute service offered by Amazon Web Services (AWS) that allows you to run code in response to various events without the need to provision or manage servers. It's designed for executing small, event-driven functions and is often used for automation, data processing, and building serverless applications.

UC4.13Use Case - Image Thumbnail Generation: Imagine you have a system that uploads images to an Amazon S3 bucket. You want to automatically generate thumbnails for these images when they are uploaded. AWS Lambda can help with this automation.

Steps:

- **Create a Lambda Function:** In the AWS Lambda Console, create a Lambda function named "GenerateThumbnail."
- **Function Code:** Write code (e.g., in Python) to extract the uploaded image, create a thumbnail, and save it back to S3.

127

- **Trigger Configuration:** Set up an S3 bucket trigger so that when new images are uploaded, the Lambda function is invoked.
- **Execution Role:** Create an IAM role that grants the Lambda function permission to access the S3 bucket and create CloudWatch logs.
- **Testing:** Upload an image to the S3 bucket, and Lambda will automatically generate a thumbnail in response.

2. AZURE LOGIC APPS:

DESCRIPTION:
Azure Logic Apps is a cloud service provided by Microsoft Azure that allows you to automate workflows and integrate services, applications, and data across cloud and on-premises environments. It provides a visual designer for building complex workflows using a wide range of connectors and triggers.

UC 4.14: USE CASE TITLE- EMAIL NOTIFICATION FOR NEW LEADS

Let's say you manage an e-commerce website and want to notify your sales team via email each time a new lead is added to your CRM system (e.g., Dynamics 365). This process can be automated using Azure Logic Apps.

STEPS:
- Create a Logic App: In the Azure Portal, create a new Logic App and use the Logic App Designer.
- Add a Trigger: Choose a trigger, such as "When a record is created" in Dynamics 365.
- Define Workflow: Build a workflow that includes actions like sending an email, formatting data, and filtering based on conditions.
- Connectors: Configure connectors for Dynamics 365 and your email service (e.g., Outlook or SendGrid).

☁ Testing: Create a new lead in Dynamics 365, and Azure Logic Apps will automatically trigger the workflow to send an email notification to your sales team.

3. GOOGLE CLOUD FUNCTIONS

DESCRIPTION:

Google Cloud Functions is a serverless compute service within Google Cloud that allows you to run single-purpose functions in response to events. It's designed for event-driven automation, data processing, and building serverless applications, similar to AWS Lambda and Azure Functions.

UC 4.15: USE CASE TITLE- REAL-TIME DATA PROCESSING:

Think about a situation where you need to analyze streaming data from IoT devices that you receive and store it in Google BigQuery. Using Google Cloud Functions, this procedure can be automated.

STEPS:

☁ Create a Cloud Function: In the Google Cloud Console, create a new Cloud Function named "ProcessIoTData."

☁ Function Code: Write code (e.g., in Node.js) to ingest, process, and store IoT data in Google BigQuery.

☁ Trigger Configuration: Set up a Cloud Pub/Sub topic as the trigger, so that when new IoT data is published to the topic, the Cloud Function is invoked.

☁ Permissions: Ensure the Cloud Function has the necessary permissions to access Cloud Pub/Sub and BigQuery.

Testing: Publish IoT data to the Pub/Sub topic, and the Cloud Function will automatically process and store the data in BigQuery.

Chapter 5:
Cloud Security

5.1. IDENTITY AND ACCESS MANAGEMENT

(IAM)

Identity and Access Management (IAM) is a critical component of cloud technology that governs who has access to cloud resources and what actions they can perform. Two fundamental aspects of IAM are Role-Based Access Control (RBAC) and Identity Providers (IdPs). Let's explore each in detail with examples.

1. ROLE-BASED ACCESS CONTROL (RBAC)

DESCRIPTION:
In IAM, RBAC is a popular access control technique where users or entities are assigned to roles and permissions are granted based on those roles. By dividing users into roles with similar responsibilities and permissions, this method makes access management simpler. In cloud computing, IAM refers to controlling access to resources and services. By allocating permissions based on roles, RBAC makes access management simpler. Identity providers authenticate users and entities to enable secure and practical access through SSO. In cloud environments, these mechanisms are crucial for preserving security and access control.

UC 5.1 USE CASE TITLE- HOW RBAC IS IMPLEMENTED?

131

Consider that you are in charge of a cloud environment on a well-known cloud provider (e.g., AWS, Azure, Google Cloud). Here is an illustration of how RBAC can be used:

- **Create Roles:** Define roles based on job functions or responsibilities. For example, create roles like "Developer," "Administrator," and "Auditor."
- **Assign Permissions:** Assign permissions to each role. Permissions specify what actions (e.g., read, write, delete) can be performed on specific resources (e.g., virtual machines, databases).
- **Assign Users/Entities to Roles:** Assign individual users, groups, or services to roles based on their responsibilities. For instance:
  - Assign developers to the "Developer" role.
  - Assign system administrators to the "Administrator" role.
  - Assign auditors to the "Auditor" role.
- **Policy Attachments:** Attach policies to roles, which define the specific permissions for that role. Policies can be predefined or custom. For example:
  - The "Developer" role might have a policy allowing read and write access to a specific S3 bucket in AWS.
  - The "Auditor" role might have a policy allowing read-only access to audit logs.
- **Effective Access Control:** Users or services assume the permissions associated with their assigned role. This ensures that each user/entity can perform only the actions allowed by their role's policies.

Benefits of RBAC:

- **Simplified Access Management:** RBAC simplifies access management by grouping users and permissions logically.
- **Scalability:** As your organization grows, it's easier to manage permissions by adding or modifying roles rather than individually assigning permissions.

☁ **Granular Control:** RBAC allows for granular control over who can perform specific actions on resources.

2. IDENTITY PROVIDERS (IDPS)

DESCRIPTION:

Identity Providers, often known as IdPs, are a type of service that authenticates and verifies the identity of people or organizations trying to gain access to cloud resources. They function as reliable sources of identity information and are at the heart of Single Sign-On (SSO) solutions, which provide users access to a variety of applications with just a single set of credentials.

UC 5.2: USE CASE TITLE- IMPLEMENT SSO USING AN IDP.

Consider a scenario where an organization uses a cloud-based SaaS application (e.g., Salesforce) and wants to implement SSO using an IdP. Here's how it works:

☁ **Identity Provider Setup:** The organization sets up an Identity Provider (e.g., Azure AD, Okta, Google Identity Platform) that will authenticate users.

☁ **Service Provider Configuration:** The SaaS application (Service Provider) is configured to trust the IdP for authentication.

☁ **User Access:** When a user attempts to access the SaaS application, they are redirected to the IdP's login page.

☁ **Authentication:** The user logs in with their credentials (e.g., username and password) on the IdP's login page.

- **Assertion:** Upon successful authentication, the IdP generates a security assertion (e.g., SAML token, JWT) containing the user's identity information.
- **Access Granted:** The IdP sends the assertion to the SaaS application, which verifies the assertion's validity with the IdP.
- **User Access Granted:** If the assertion is valid, the SaaS application grants the user access, allowing them to use the application without providing separate credentials.

Benefits of Identity Providers:

- **Single Sign-On (SSO):** IdPs enable SSO, improving user experience by reducing the need to remember multiple sets of credentials.
- **Centralized Authentication:** Authentication is centralized with the IdP, enhancing security and simplifying access management.
- **Multi-Factor Authentication (MFA):** Many IdPs support MFA, adding an extra layer of security.
- **Federation:** IdPs facilitate trust relationships between organizations, enabling secure access to shared resources.

5.2. NETWORK SECURITY

A key component of cloud technology is network security, which guarantees the protection of cloud resources and data from unauthorized access, cyberattacks, and other security risks. The protection of cloud resources and data depends on network security. A thorough network security strategy must include firewalls, security groups, and DDoS protection because they help organizations reduce security risks and guarantee the availability and integrity of their cloud-based services.

Firewalls, Security Groups, and DDoS (Distributed Denial of Service) defense are three essential elements of network security in the cloud. Let's investigate each in depth using examples.

CLOUD EMPOWERMENT

1. FIREWALLS:

DESCRIPTION:

Firewalls are network security devices or software that monitor and control incoming and outgoing network traffic based on predetermined security rules. They act as barriers between trusted and untrusted networks, allowing or blocking traffic based on defined policies.

UC 5.3: USE CASE TITLE- HOW TO USE FIREWALLS TO ENHANCE NETWORK SECURITY.

Consider yourself the manager of a web application that runs in the cloud on a platform like AWS, Azure, or Google Cloud. The following are some ways that firewalls can improve network security:

- **Network ACLs (AWS, Azure) or Security Groups (AWS):** These are cloud-specific firewall tools that allow you to control inbound and outbound traffic to your cloud resources.

Scenario: You want to secure your web application hosted on AWS by allowing only HTTP (port 80) and HTTPS (port 443) traffic to reach your web servers. All other incoming traffic should be blocked.

- **Firewall Configuration:**
  - o In AWS, you can create a Security Group for your web servers.
  - o Define inbound rules allowing traffic on ports 80 and 443 from specific IP ranges (e.g., from the Internet or a specific set of trusted IP addresses).
  - o Configure outbound rules as needed, such as allowing web servers to communicate with a database server on a specific port.
  - o Apply the Security Group to your web server instances.

135

☁ **Result:** With this firewall configuration, only HTTP and HTTPS traffic from allowed sources will reach your web servers, providing protection against unauthorized access.

Benefits of Firewalls:

☁ **Traffic Control:** Firewalls allow fine-grained control over traffic entering and leaving your network, helping to prevent unauthorized access and attacks.

☁ **Security Policy Enforcement:** They enforce security policies consistently across your network, reducing the risk of configuration errors.

☁ **Protection Against Threats:** Firewalls can protect against common threats like port scanning, intrusion attempts, and unauthorized access.

2. SECURITY GROUPS:

DESCRIPTION:

Security Groups are a type of firewall provided by cloud service providers (e.g., AWS, Azure, Google Cloud). They are used to control inbound and outbound traffic to and from cloud resources such as virtual machines (VMs) and database instances.

UC 5.4: USE CASE TITLE: SECURITY GROUP CONFIGURATION (GOOGLE CLOUD)

Suppose you are responsible for securing a set of virtual machines (VMs) in Google Cloud. You want to allow SSH access only from a specific IP address range to enhance security.

Security Group Configuration (Google Cloud):

☁ Create a Security Group for your VM instances.

☁ Define an ingress rule allowing traffic on port 22 (SSH) from your specified IP address range.

☁ Associate the Security Group with your VM instances.

CLOUD EMPOWERMENT

Result: Only SSH traffic from the specified IP address range will be allowed to reach the VM instances, reducing the attack surface and potential security risks.

Benefits of Security Groups:

- **Simplified Rule Management:** Security Groups simplify rule management by allowing you to define rules at the instance level.
- **Dynamic Rule Updates:** Changes to Security Group rules take effect immediately, enhancing flexibility and agility.
- **Defense in Depth:** By using Security Groups in conjunction with other security measures, you can create a defense-in-depth strategy.

3. DDOS PROTECTION:

DESCRIPTION:

DDoS protection involves measures to defend against Distributed Denial of Service attacks, where multiple compromised devices are used to flood a target system with traffic, causing it to become overwhelmed and unavailable.

UC5.5: USE CASE TITLE: HOW TO USE DDOS PROTECTION SERVICE?

Suppose you are running a critical web application on a cloud platform like AWS. To protect your application from DDoS attacks, you can use AWS Shield, a DDoS protection service provided by AWS.

AWS Shield Configuration:

- Enable AWS Shield Standard or Advanced for your web application.
- AWS Shield Standard provides automatic protection against common DDoS attacks.

- AWS Shield Advanced offers enhanced protection and real-time attack visibility.
- Configure protection policies based on your application's needs.

Result: AWS Shield will detect and mitigate DDoS attacks, ensuring that your web application remains accessible to legitimate users even during an attack.

Benefits of DDoS Protection:

- **Mitigation of Attacks:** DDoS protection services like AWS Shield actively monitor and mitigate DDoS attacks, keeping your services available.
- **Traffic Scrubbing:** They filter out malicious traffic and allow legitimate traffic to reach your resources.
- **Real-time Monitoring:** Advanced DDoS protection services provide real-time visibility into ongoing attacks, allowing for timely responses.

5.3. DATA SECURITY

When using cloud computing, data security is crucial to preventing breaches and unauthorized access to sensitive data. Key Management and Encryption at Rest and in Transit are two essential components of cloud data security. Encryption both in transit and at rest is necessary for cloud data security, as is efficient key management. These steps help organizations comply with regulations by securing data from unauthorized access, guaranteeing its confidentiality, and maintaining its integrity. A solid and secure cloud data security strategy must properly implement encryption and key management. Let's investigate each in depth using examples.

1. ENCRYPTION AT REST AND IN TRANSIT:

DESCRIPTION:

- **Encryption at Rest:** This involves encrypting data when it is stored or "at rest" in storage systems, databases, or other data repositories. Even if an attacker gains access to the physical storage media, the data remains protected.
- **Encryption in Transit:** This pertains to encrypting data while it is being transmitted between systems or across networks. It ensures that data remains confidential and intact during transmission.

UC 5.6: USE CASE TITLE- DATA IS ENCRYPTED BOTH AT REST AND IN TRANSIT.

Consider storing sensitive customer data in a cloud-based database service (like AWS RDS, Azure SQL Database, or Google Cloud SQL). Make sure the data is encrypted both at rest and while being transmitted.

Encryption at Rest Configuration (AWS RDS):

- Enable encryption for your RDS instance when creating it or modifying its settings.
- RDS will automatically use AWS Key Management Service (KMS) to generate and manage encryption keys.
- All data stored in the RDS instance, including backups, will be encrypted with the KMS-generated key.

Encryption in Transit Configuration (AWS RDS):

- Configure your database client applications to connect to the RDS instance using SSL/TLS.
- Ensure that the database engine parameter group includes settings to enforce SSL connections.

- Data transmitted between your application and the RDS instance will be encrypted during transit.

Benefits of Encryption at Rest and in Transit:

- **Confidentiality:** Encryption ensures that even if data is accessed without authorization, it remains unreadable.
- **Data Integrity:** It verifies that data hasn't been tampered with during storage or transmission.
- **Regulatory Compliance:** Many data protection regulations require data encryption.

2. KEY MANAGEMENT

DESCRIPTION:

Key management involves the generation, storage, distribution, rotation, and revocation of encryption keys. Proper key management is essential to maintain the security of encrypted data. Cloud service providers often offer Key Management Services (KMS) to simplify key management tasks.

UC 5.7: USE CASE TITLE- USING ENCRYPTION KEY.

Take for example the fact that you are using Amazon S3 to store sensitive company documents. You need to make sure that the encryption keys that are being used to protect these documents are being managed in a secure manner.

Key Management Configuration (AWS KMS):

- Create a customer master key (CMK) in AWS Key Management Service (KMS).
- Assign appropriate permissions to the CMK to control who can use it for encryption and decryption.
- Configure your S3 buckets to use the CMK for server-side encryption.

☁ Enable automatic rotation of keys to enhance security.

Key Rotation:

☁ Set up key rotation policies in AWS KMS to automatically generate new encryption keys at regular intervals.

☁ When a key is rotated, it doesn't affect data that was encrypted with the old key; decryption can still occur transparently.

Benefits of Key Management:

☁ **Security:** Proper key management ensures that encryption keys are stored and handled securely.

☁ **Granular Control:** Key management allows organizations to control who can access data by managing access to encryption keys.

☁ **Compliance:** Key management helps organizations meet regulatory requirements for data security.

5.4. COMPLIANCE AND GOVERNANCE

Compliance and governance in cloud technology are essential for ensuring that organizations adhere to the industry-specific regulations and follow best practices to safeguard data, keep the system secure, and fulfill legal requirements. The terms "compliance" and "governance" in the context of cloud computing refer to the process of adhering to sector-specific regulations and putting cloud security best practices into action. These efforts are necessary for ensuring compliance with legal requirements, protecting sensitive data, and keeping systems secure. Building secure and reliable cloud environments for their operations is possible for businesses when they combine regulatory compliance with security best practices. Regulatory Compliance and Cloud Security Best Practices are Two Key Aspects of Compliance and Governance in the

141

Cloud Regulatory Compliance. Let's look at each of these in greater depth by providing some examples.

1. REGULATORY COMPLIANCE:

DESCRIPTION:

Regulatory compliance is the process of ensuring that an organization's cloud operations and data management practices are in accordance with applicable industry-specific regulations, laws, and standards. This process is referred to as regulatory compliance. Compliance requirements are subject to change based on factors such as the sector, location, and nature of the data that is being managed.

UC 5.8: USE CASE TITLE: HIPAA COMPLIANCE IN HEALTHCARE

Imagine you work for a healthcare company that stores patient records in the cloud. You have access to those records from anywhere. You are going to need to do the following in order to stay in compliance with the Health Insurance Portability and Accountability Act (HIPAA):

- **Data Encryption:** Ensure that patient data is encrypted both at rest and in transit. Use encryption services provided by your cloud provider (e.g., AWS KMS, Azure Key Vault) to protect sensitive information.
- **Access Controls:** Implement strict access controls to ensure that only authorized personnel can access patient records. Use Role-Based Access Control (RBAC) and Multi-Factor Authentication (MFA) to secure access.
- **Audit Trails:** Enable auditing and monitoring to track who accessed patient data and when. Use cloud-native auditing services or third-party solutions to maintain detailed audit logs.
- **Data Retention:** Establish data retention policies to ensure that patient records are retained for the required period and securely disposed of when no longer needed.

- **Incident Response:** Develop an incident response plan to address data breaches promptly. This should include notification procedures, reporting to regulatory authorities, and corrective actions.
- **Regular Auditing:** Conduct regular internal and external audits to assess compliance with HIPAA regulations. Use tools and third-party auditors to evaluate your security measures.

Benefits of Regulatory Compliance:

- **Legal Protection:** Compliance helps organizations avoid legal penalties, fines, and reputational damage.
- **Data Security:** It ensures that sensitive data is adequately protected, reducing the risk of data breaches.
- **Trust and Reputation:** Compliant organizations build trust with customers and partners, enhancing their reputation.

2. CLOUD SECURITY BEST PRACTICES:

DESCRIPTION:

Best practices for cloud security are comprised of a collection of guidelines, configurations, and strategies that have been developed to improve the safety of cloud-based environments. These practices are not specific to any one particular regulation; rather, they are fundamental principles for protecting one's data and resources while they are stored in the cloud.

UC 5.9: USE CASE TITLE- CLOUD SECURITY BEST PRACTICES

Regardless of the industry or regulatory requirements, organizations should implement cloud security best practices, such as:

- **Identity and Access Management (IAM):** Implement strict IAM policies, including RBAC, MFA, and principle of least privilege, to control access to cloud resources.
- **Data Encryption:** Use encryption at rest and in transit for all sensitive data. Encrypt data before it leaves your premises and decrypt it only when necessary.
- **Continuous Monitoring:** Implement continuous monitoring and alerting to detect and respond to security threats in real-time. Use cloud-native monitoring tools or third-party solutions.
- **Security Patch Management:** Regularly update and patch cloud resources, including virtual machines, containers, and serverless functions, to protect against known vulnerabilities.
- **Backup and Disaster Recovery:** Implement automated backup and disaster recovery plans to ensure data availability in case of unexpected events.
- **Network Security:** Use firewalls, security groups, and network access controls to segment and secure your cloud network. Implement intrusion detection and prevention systems.
- **Logging and Auditing:** Enable comprehensive logging and auditing of cloud activities. Analyze logs for security incidents and maintain audit trails.

Benefits of Cloud Security Best Practices:

- **Proactive Defense:** Best practices help organizations proactively defend against security threats, reducing the likelihood of breaches.
- **Cost Efficiency:** Implementing best practices can help organizations avoid costly security incidents and downtime.
- **Compliance Alignment:** Many Cloud security best practices align with regulatory compliance requirements, simplifying compliance efforts.

Chapter 6
Cloud Cost Management

6.1. BILLING MODELS

The management of cloud costs is an essential component of making effective use of cloud services while maintaining financial discipline. Cloud service providers make available a wide range of billing models to cater to the diverse requirements of their customers.

The various Cloud Cost Management Billing Models, such as Pay-as-you-go, Reserved Instances (RIs), and Spot Instances, each provide their own unique strategy for the provisioning and optimization of cloud resources at the lowest possible cost. The nature of your workloads, the limitations of your budget, and the demands placed on your resources all play a role in the decision of which model to use.

Organizations are able to maximize their cloud spending while still satisfying their operational requirements if they have a solid understanding of the various billing models and the use cases for each of them. As was mentioned earlier, Pay-as-you-go billing,

Reserved Instances (RIs), and Spot Instances are three common types of billing models. Let's look at some real-world examples of each of these.

1. PAY-AS-YOU-GO

DESCRIPTION:
Pay-as-you-go is a flexible billing model that allows users to pay for cloud resources on an hourly or per-minute basis, depending on the cloud provider. Pay-as-you-go billing models are becoming increasingly popular. Because you are only billed for the resources you actually make

145

use of with this model, it is ideally suited for workloads that make unpredictable or variable use of their resources.

UC 6.1: USE CASE TITLE- PAY-AS-YOU-GO.

Imagine that you are a newly established business that has just released a brand-new web application. In the beginning, there are not many people using your system, so your resource consumption is relatively low. In a model known as pay-as-you-go:

- **Resource Provisioning:** You deploy virtual machines (VMs) and databases in the cloud.
- **Billing:** You are billed based on the actual usage of these resources, which is low in the early stages.
- **Scaling:** As your application gains popularity, you can easily scale up resources to accommodate increased demand.
- **Billing Adjustment:** Your bills increase proportionally to the additional resources you use, ensuring cost-effectiveness.

Benefits of Pay-as-you-go:

- **Flexibility:** You can start and stop resources as needed, adapting to changing workloads.
- **No Upfront Costs:** There are no upfront payments or long-term commitments.
- **Cost Control:** Pay-as-you-go offers cost transparency and control, making it suitable for startups and small businesses.

2. RESERVED INSTANCES (RIS):

DESCRIPTION:

Reserved Instances, or RIs, enable users to make a financial commitment to a predetermined quantity of cloud resources for a predetermined period of time (typically between one and three years) in exchange for significant cost savings when compared to pay-as-you-go rates. RIs are the best option for workloads that are consistent and predictable.

UC 6.2: Use Case Title- Reserved Instances.

Imagine that you run a business that maintains a database that is essential to the operation of the company in the cloud. You are aware that there will be consistent use of this database over the course of the next three years. In a model with RI:

- **RI Purchase:** You purchase RIs for the specific instance type, region, and term (e.g., three years) matching your database requirements.
- **Billing:** You are billed a lower hourly rate compared to pay-as-you-go for the reserved capacity.
- **Cost Savings:** Over the three-year term, you realize substantial cost savings compared to paying the higher pay-as-you-go rates.
- **Resource Utilization:** Your database resources are continuously available, ensuring high availability and performance.

Benefits of Reserved Instances:

- **Cost Savings:** RIs offer significant cost savings compared to pay-as-you-go for stable workloads.
- **Resource Guarantee:** You have guaranteed access to resources, ensuring performance and availability.
- **Budget Predictability:** RIs provide budget predictability for long-term projects and enterprise workloads.

3. SPOT INSTANCES:

DESCRIPTION:

Spot Instances provide users with the opportunity to bid on spare cloud capacity at prices that are significantly lower than those of pay-as-you-go rates. Nevertheless, the cloud provider has the ability to terminate these instances with very little notice in the event that the capacity is required elsewhere. Workloads that can tolerate errors and are not particularly time sensitive should be run on spot instances.

UC 6.3: USE CASE TITLE- SPOT INSTANCE
MODEL

Imagine that you run a pipeline for processing large amounts of data that is capable of being distributed across multiple nodes. You are looking to reduce costs, but the processing time is not an absolute necessity. In a model called a Spot Instance:

- **Spot Instance Request:** You request Spot Instances for the required number of processing nodes, specifying your bid price.
- **Billing:** You are billed at the current Spot price, which is usually significantly lower than pay-as-you-go rates.
- **Cost Savings:** You achieve substantial cost savings by using Spot Instances for your batch processing.
- **Termination:** Occasionally, instances may be terminated if the Spot price rises or if the capacity is needed elsewhere, but this is acceptable for your fault-tolerant workload.

Benefits of Spot Instances:

- **Cost Efficiency:** Spot Instances offer the lowest cost per unit of computing power.
- **Scalability:** You can rapidly scale your workload when spare capacity is available.
- **Use Cases:** Spot Instances are suitable for fault-tolerant applications, batch processing, and high-performance computing tasks.

6.2. COST OPTIMIZATION STRATEGIES

Management of cloud costs is an essential business practice for companies that use cloud services. This allows companies to maximize their profits while minimizing unnecessary expenditures and ensuring they have sufficient resources to fulfill all of their requirements. Management of cloud costs is essential for businesses looking to get the most out of their cloud investments. Organizations are provided with the ability to optimize spending, more accurately allocate costs, and improve resource management when they implement strategies such as "right-sizing" resources, "tagging" and "resource grouping," and "using cost monitoring tools." These practices contribute to the efficient operation of the cloud as well as the cost-effective usage of the cloud. The right sizing of resources, proper tagging and grouping of resources, and the use of cost monitoring tools are the three most important cost optimization strategies for cloud cost management. In order to better understand each of these, let's look at some examples.

1. RIGHT-SIZING RESOURCES:

DESCRIPTION:
Right-sizing resources involves ensuring that cloud resources, such as virtual machines (VMs) and databases, are appropriately sized to match the workload's requirements. This strategy helps avoid over-provisioning (paying for resources that are underutilized) and under-provisioning (causing performance issues).

UC 6.4: USE CASE TITLE- RIGHT SIZING

RESOURCES

Imagine that you are hosting your web application on Amazon Web Services (AWS), and that you have multiple EC2 instances to attend to the needs of the people who visit your website. You initially provisioned instances with substantial amounts of both CPU and memory because you anticipated a high volume of traffic. This was a smart move on your part. However, as a result of monitoring the application's usage, you have

149

come to the realization that your program rarely uses more than forty percent of the resources that are readily available.

Right-sizing Strategy:

- Analyze the CPU and memory utilization of your EC2 instances using AWS CloudWatch or similar monitoring tools.
- Identify instances that are consistently underutilized.
- Downsize those instances to a smaller instance type that better matches the actual workload requirements.

Result:

- By right-sizing your EC2 instances, you reduce your compute costs while maintaining adequate performance.
- For instance, you may move from a c5.4xlarge instance to a c5.large instance, saving costs without sacrificing performance.

Benefits of Right-sizing Resources:

- **Cost Savings:** Right-sizing eliminates the cost of unused resources.
- **Performance Optimization:** It ensures resources are appropriately matched to workload demands.
- **Budget Efficiency:** Organizations can allocate their cloud budgets more effectively.

2. TAGGING AND RESOURCE GROUPING:

DESCRIPTION:

The process of tagging and resource grouping involves first assigning metadata to cloud resources in the form of tags, and then organizing, searching, and managing cloud resources according to the tags that have been assigned. This strategy improves both visibility and the distribution of costs.

UC 6.5: USE CASE TITLE- TAGGING & RESOURCE GROUPING.

CLOUD EMPOWERMENT

Imagine that you are the IT manager for your organization and that you are responsible for a number of departments, each of which uses cloud resources. For the purpose of accurately allocating costs and effectively managing resources:

Tagging Strategy:

- Assign tags to resources, such as department, project, environment (production, development, staging), and owner.
- Ensure consistency in tagging practices across your organization.

Resource Grouping:

- Use cloud management tools to create resource groups based on tags (e.g., "Production," "Development," "Marketing").
- Generate cost reports and budget allocation based on these resource groups.

Result:

- You can track and allocate costs accurately to each department or project based on tags.
- Resource groups allow you to manage and monitor resources within logical categories.

Benefits of Tagging and Resource Grouping:

- **Cost Allocation:** Accurate cost attribution to departments or projects simplifies budgeting.
- **Resource Management:** It enhances resource visibility and management.
- **Compliance:** Tagging can help ensure resources are used according to organizational policies.

3. COST MONITORING TOOLS:

DESCRIPTION:

Cloud-native or third-party solutions can be used as cost monitoring tools. These tools provide visibility into cloud spending as well as cloud usage. These tools assist organizations in analyzing patterns of spending, establishing budgets, and locating opportunities to save money on costs.

UC 6.6: USE CASE TITLE- COST MONITORING IN GCP

Suppose you are a cloud administrator responsible for managing costs in your Google Cloud environment:

Cost Monitoring Tool Strategy:

- Implement Google Cloud's built-in cost management tools like Google Cloud Cost Explorer and Billing Reports.
- Configure budgets and alerts to receive notifications when spending exceeds predefined thresholds.

Result:

- You gain insights into your Google Cloud spending patterns through detailed cost reports and visualizations.
- Budget alerts notify you when spending exceeds expectations, allowing you to take corrective actions promptly.

Benefits of Cost Monitoring Tools:

- **Visibility:** Detailed cost and usage reports provide insights into cloud spending.
- **Budget Control:** Alerts and budgets help organizations stay within financial constraints.
- **Optimization:** Cost monitoring tools highlight areas where cost savings can be achieved.

CLOUD EMPOWERMENT

Chapter 7
Cloud Migration and Adoption

7.1. CLOUD MIGRATION STRATEGIES

Cloud migration is the process of moving an organization's data, applications, and workloads from an environment that is hosted on-premises or by another cloud provider to an environment that is hosted in the cloud. This can be done by moving the data centers themselves to the cloud. Migrating to the cloud can be accomplished in a variety of ways, each of which offers its own distinct set of advantages as well as concerns to take into account. Migration strategies to the cloud should be selected with consideration given to the particular objectives, resources, and constraints of an organization. Lift and Shift is an approach that enables a rapid migration, Re-platforming makes it possible to reap some of the benefits of the cloud, and Re-factoring fully embraces the cloud's native capabilities. The current state of the application and the anticipated benefits of the cloud migration should guide the selection of the appropriate strategy. There are several common strategies, including "lift and shift," "re-platforming," and "re-factoring." Another common tactic is known as the lift and shift. Let's look at some real-life examples of each of these things, shall we?

1. LIFT AND SHIFT:

DESCRIPTION:
Lift and Shift is a migration strategy that is also known as Re-hosting. It is used by companies when they want to move their existing applications and workloads to the cloud with as few modifications as possible. With this strategy, the goal is to complete the migration in a short amount of time while minimizing the number of changes made to the underlying application architecture.

CLOUD EMPOWERMENT

Imagine you have a legacy web application running on physical servers in your on-premises data center. The application uses a monolithic architecture and relies on a traditional relational database. In a Lift and Shift scenario:

Migration Process:

- ☁ You choose a cloud provider (e.g., AWS, Azure, Google Cloud) and provision virtual machines (VMs) with similar configurations to your on-premises servers.
- ☁ You install the same operating system and middleware on the cloud VMs.
- ☁ You migrate the application code and data to the cloud VMs, ensuring compatibility.

Result:

- ☁ The application now runs in the cloud without major changes.
- ☁ While this approach may not fully leverage cloud-native features, it provides a quick and cost-effective way to move to the cloud.

Benefits of Lift and Shift:

- ☁ Speed: It's one of the fastest migration strategies since it involves minimal application changes.
- ☁ Low Risk: Since the application remains largely unchanged, there's a lower risk of introducing new bugs or issues during migration.
- ☁ Immediate Cloud Benefits: You gain immediate access to cloud infrastructure, scalability, and reliability.

2. RE-PLATFORMING

DESCRIPTION:

Re-platforming, also known as Lift, Tinker, and Shift, entails making a few tweaks to an application while it is being migrated to the cloud in order to make use of some cloud-native features without having to completely re-architect the application. These tweaks can be made in order to take advantage of some cloud-native features.

UC 7.2: USE CASE TITLE - RE-PLATFORMING SCENARIO.

Imagine that you already have an application written in Java and that you want to move it to the cloud. Within the context of a Re-platforming scenario:

Migration Process:

- You move the application to a cloud-based VM with a similar configuration.
- You may upgrade the database to a cloud-native database service like Amazon RDS (for AWS) or Azure SQL Database (for Azure).
- You make minor code adjustments to take advantage of cloud scalability, such as optimizing database queries for the cloud database service.

Result:

- The application runs in the cloud with improved scalability and reliability.
- You leverage some cloud-native features while maintaining most of the existing application code.

Benefits of Re-platforming:

- Improved Scalability: Applications can take advantage of cloud resources and scalability.

CLOUD EMPOWERMENT

☁ Cost Savings: You can optimize costs by using cloud-native database services.

☁ Enhanced Reliability: Cloud infrastructure often provides better availability and redundancy.

2. RE-FACTORING

DESCRIPTION:

Re-factoring, also known as re-architecting, is a migration strategy in which businesses make significant changes to their applications in order to fully leverage cloud-native features. Re-factoring is also sometimes referred to as re-engineering. This strategy frequently involves separating monolithic applications into smaller microservices or employing serverless computing.

UC 7.3: USE CASE TITLE- RE-FACTORING

SCENARIO.

Imagine you have a legacy monolithic application that has components that are tightly coupled to one another. Within the context of a Refactoring scenario:

Migration Process:

☁ You analyze the application and identify components that can be decoupled and run independently.

☁ You re-architect the application to use microservices or serverless functions.

☁ You leverage cloud-native services like AWS Lambda (for AWS), Azure Functions (for Azure), or Google Cloud Functions (for Google Cloud).

Result:

- The application is now highly scalable, resilient, and cost-efficient.
- You take full advantage of cloud-native features and can auto-scale individual components as needed.

Benefits of Re-factoring:

- Cloud-Native Benefits: Applications are fully optimized for the cloud, benefiting from scalability, reliability, and cost-effectiveness.
- Future-Proofing: Re-factoring allows organizations to stay competitive by modernizing their applications.
- Microservices: Applications can be more easily maintained and updated as individual microservices.

7.2. CLOUD ADOPTION BEST PRACTICES

The process of an organization adopting cloud computing is a transformative journey that involves more than just the implementation of technical aspects. In order to ensure a smooth transition to the cloud, it is necessary to give careful consideration to change management practices, as well as training and upskilling procedures. Let's investigate these recommended procedures by looking at some examples.

1. CHANGE MANAGEMENT:

DESCRIPTION:
The process of planning, implementing, and overseeing the management of changes within an organization is referred to as change management. In the context of adopting cloud computing, this refers to the process of preparing an organization and all of its personnel for the transition to cloud-based technologies, procedures, and practices.

UC 7.4: USE CASE TITLE- CHANGE MANAGEMENT

CLOUD EMPOWERMENT

Imagine a medium-sized manufacturing company that decides to migrate its on-premises data center to a cloud environment (e.g., AWS, Azure) (e.g., AWS, Azure). Here's how change management can be applied:

- **Evaluation and Planning:** In order to get a better understanding of how the transition to the cloud will affect the company's operations, processes, and employees, the company carries out an evaluation.

- **Engagement of Stakeholders:** Key stakeholders, such as executives, IT teams, and end-users, are involved in the planning process at an early stage in order to gain their buy-in and address any concerns they may have.

- **Communication:** The company shares with all of its staff members the objectives and advantages of migrating to the cloud through a variety of different channels, including emails, meetings, and updates posted on the intranet.

- **Training:** Educating employees on the new cloud technologies and tools they will be using is a priority, so training sessions are regularly planned and carried out. This includes education on the most effective cloud security practices.

- **Testing:** Before beginning a migration on a larger scale, the company first performs a series of pilot migrations and testing phases to locate and address any problems or concerns that may arise.

- **Feedback and Adaptation:** During the entire migration process, feedback from employees is continuously gathered, and adjustments are made based on their suggestions and recommendations.

- **Support:** Adequate support mechanisms are put into place, such as helpdesk support and documentation, in order to assist employees both during and after the migration process.

- **Monitoring and Evaluation:** After the migration has been completed, the company will monitor performance and solicit feedback in order to determine how successful the migration was and how they can improve it further.

Benefits of Change Management:

- **Smooth Transition:** Change management helps organizations navigate the transition to the cloud with minimal disruption to operations.
- **Employee Adoption:** Engaging employees and providing proper training increases their comfort and proficiency with cloud technologies.
- **Risk Mitigation:** It helps identify and address potential challenges early, reducing the risk of project delays and failures.

2. TRAINING AND UPSKILLING

DESCRIPTION

Employees are provided with the knowledge and skills necessary to make effective use of cloud technologies and to make the most of the capabilities offered by the cloud through a process known as training and upskilling.

UC 7.5: USE CASE TITLE- TRAINING & UPSKILLING

Take, for example, a company that provides financial services and is in the process of migrating its data analytics platform to the cloud (e.g., Google Cloud Platform). Increasing one's level of expertise and training can be applied in the following ways:

- **Evaluation of Skills:** In order to determine where there are deficiencies, the company evaluates the existing skills and knowledge of its data analytics team.
- **Plan of Instruction Tailored to Each Team Member:** Based on Their Role and Skill Gaps A tailored plan of instruction is

devised for each member of the team. For instance, data analysts could receive training in the use of Google BigQuery, while data engineers could receive training in the orchestration of data pipelines using Cloud Composer.

- **Certification** is something that employees are strongly encouraged to pursue at this particular company. Examples of relevant certifications include Google Cloud Professional Data Engineer and Amazon Web Services Certified Solutions Architect.

- **Hands-On Labs:** Employees are given the opportunity to participate in labs and exercises that are both hands-on and practical, so that they can put what they've learned into practice.

- **Ongoing Education:** Ongoing education is encouraged through the use of online courses, webinars, and access to documentation provided by cloud service providers.

- **Mentoring and Information Exchange:** Experienced members of the team take on the role of mentors, assisting less-skilled members of the team in their education and discussing the most effective methods.

- **Monitoring Progress:** The business frequently evaluates the level of progress made by members of the team in the acquisition of cloud skills and modifies the training plans accordingly.

Benefits of Training and Upskilling:

- **Advantage in the Market:** Having a competent workforce that is able to tap into the full potential offered by cloud technologies provides an organization with an advantage in the market.

- **Productivity:** Employees who have received adequate training are more productive and are better able to efficiently solve problems.

- **Employee retention** can be improved by investing in employee development, which also increases job satisfaction for employees and can help retain employees.

Chapter 8:
Advanced Cloud Topics

8.1. BIG DATA AND ANALYTICS IN THE CLOUD

The collection, storage, processing, and analysis of massive amounts of data in the cloud by organizations has been revolutionized by Big Data and Analytics, allowing for organizations to gain valuable insights and make more informed decisions. Technologies such as data lakes, data warehouses, and a wide variety of analytics services are the driving forces behind this transformation. Let's look at some real-world examples of each.

1. DATA LAKES AND DATA WAREHOUSES:

DESCRIPTION:
Both data lakes and data warehouses are examples of storage solutions that were developed for the purpose of managing and processing large volumes of structured and unstructured data. Because of this, data lakes and data warehouses are essential components of modern Big Data and Analytics in the cloud.

- **Data Lake:** A data lake is a centralized repository that stores raw data from a variety of sources, most of the time in the format in which the source data was originally stored. It enables businesses to store and manage enormous amounts of data in a manner that is both efficient and cost-effective. Amazon S3 and Microsoft Azure Data Lake Storage are two well-known examples of popular cloud-based data lake solutions.

☁ **Data Warehouse:** On the other hand, a data warehouse is a database that is both highly organized and structured, and it is designed to be optimal for analytical querying. It brings together information from a variety of sources and stores it in a single location so that it can be analyzed. Amazon Redshift, Google BigQuery, and Azure Synapse Analytics are a few examples of cloud data warehouses.

UC 8.1: USE CASE TITLE- DATA LAKE & DATA WAREHOUSE

Let's consider a retail company that operates both physical stores and an e-commerce platform. The company collects vast amounts of data, including sales transactions, customer interactions, and supply chain data. Here's how data lakes and data warehouses can be used:

☁ **Data Lake:** Raw data from various sources, such as point-of-sale systems, online sales, and supplier data, is ingested into the data lake. This data includes structured data like sales records and unstructured data like customer reviews and social media data. The data lake stores this data efficiently, allowing the company to retain all the raw data for future analysis.

☁ **Data Warehouse:** The company's analytics team uses a cloud data warehouse to aggregate and transform the data from the data lake into a structured format suitable for analysis. For example, they create a consolidated sales data table with information on products, stores, and customer demographics. Analysts can then use SQL queries or BI tools to run complex analyses on this data, such as identifying sales trends, optimizing inventory, and personalizing marketing campaigns.

Benefits of Data Lakes and Data Warehouses:

☁ Scalability: Cloud-based solutions can scale to accommodate growing data volumes.

☁ Cost Efficiency: Pay-as-you-go pricing models in the cloud offer cost-effective data storage and processing.

CLOUD EMPOWERMENT

☁ Flexibility: Data lakes can store diverse data types, while data warehouses provide structured, query-optimized storage.

2. ANALYTICS SERVICES:

DESCRIPTION:

Cloud providers offer a wide range of analytics services that enable organizations to perform advanced analytics, machine learning, and business intelligence without managing the underlying infrastructure.

Example Services:

☁ **AWS Analytics:** Amazon offers services like Amazon EMR for big data processing, Amazon SageMaker for machine learning, and Amazon QuickSight for business intelligence and data visualization.

☁ **Azure Analytics:** Microsoft provides services such as Azure Databricks for big data analytics, Azure Machine Learning for machine learning, and Power BI for business intelligence and reporting.

☁ **Google Cloud Analytics:** Google Cloud offers solutions like Google Dataflow for data processing, BigQuery for data warehousing and analytics, and AutoML for machine learning.

UC 8.2: USE CASE TITLE- CLOUD-BASED ANALYTICS SERVICES

Let's consider a healthcare provider using cloud-based analytics services:

☁ **Data Processing:** The healthcare provider will collect patient data, such as electronic health records, medical images, and sensor data. This information will then be processed. They preprocess and clean this data at scale using cloud-based data

165

processing services such as Amazon's Elastic Map Reduce (EMR).

- **Analytics and Machine Learning:** In order to develop predictive models for patient outcomes, the healthcare provider utilizes cloud-based machine learning services such as Azure Machine Learning. These models can assist in identifying patients who are at risk of developing certain conditions, which makes it possible to take preventative measures.

- **Data Visualization:** The service provider makes use of a business intelligence tool that is hosted in the cloud, such as Power BI, to develop interactive dashboards and reports for medical professionals. These dashboards offer insights into patient demographics, the efficacy of treatment, and the utilization of resources, which helps in decision-making and improves patient care.

Benefits of Analytics Services:

- Reduced Complexity: Cloud-managed services abstract infrastructure management, allowing organizations to focus on analytics and insights.

- Scalability: Services can scale dynamically to handle increasing data volumes and analytical workloads.

- Integration: Analytics services often integrate seamlessly with other cloud services and data sources.

Big Data and Analytics conducted in the cloud provide businesses with the ability to harness the power of data, allowing them to make decisions that are more informed, gain insights, and propel innovation. Cloud providers enable businesses to more effectively store, process, analyze, and visualize data by providing services such as data lakes, data warehouses, and analytics. This, in turn, leads to improved business outcomes.

8.2. INTERNET OF THINGS (IOT) AND CLOUD

The integration of Internet of Things (IoT) and cloud computing is transforming industries by enabling the collection, processing, and analysis of massive volumes of data generated by IoT devices. This fusion relies on IoT architecture and IoT platforms to efficiently manage and make sense of the data. Let's explore these components with an example.

1. IOT ARCHITECTURE:

DESCRIPTION:

The term "Internet of Things architecture" (IoT architecture) refers to the structure and design of the system that enables communication and data flow between cloud-based services and devices that are part of the Internet of Things (IoT). The following are examples of the layers that it typically consists of:

- **Sensors and Devices:** These are the physical Internet of Things devices, such as sensors, cameras, and actuators, which collect data from the physical world. For example, the temperature of a room can be measured using a sensor.
- **Connectivity** is the name of the layer that contains all of the communication protocols and network configurations that are necessary to send data from Internet of Things devices to the cloud. MQTT, HTTP, and CoAP are all examples of common protocols. IoT gateways are frequently involved in the process of data aggregation and transmission.
- **Cloud services** include the processing, storing, and analyzing of data in the cloud itself. Databases, data processing tools, machine learning algorithms, and application hosting environments are some examples of what can be included in cloud services.

167

☁ **Application and Analytics:** This layer is comprised of applications and services that extract insights from the information collected by IoT devices. Dashboards, predictive maintenance algorithms, and real-time alerts are some examples of this type of software.

UC 8.3: USE CASE TITLE- TRAFFIC MANAGEMENT USING IoT AND CLOUD TECHNOLOGY.

Consider a project for a smart city that utilizes the internet of things and cloud computing in order to improve the efficiency of traffic management:

- **Sensors and Devices:** Traffic cameras, vehicle detectors, and weather sensors are deployed across the city to collect data on traffic conditions, vehicle counts, and weather conditions.

- **Connectivity:** Data from these sensors is transmitted over a cellular network to a centralized IoT gateway, which aggregates and forwards the data to the cloud.

- **Cloud Services:** In the cloud, data is ingested into a data lake or database, where it is stored and processed. Big data processing tools like Apache Spark may be used to clean and transform the data.

- **Application and Analytics:** Traffic management applications and analytics services analyze the data in real-time. For instance, machine learning models can predict traffic congestion, and city officials can adjust traffic signals or send alerts to commuters through mobile apps.

Benefits of IoT Architecture:

☁ **Scalability:** IoT architecture can accommodate the deployment of a vast number of devices and the processing of large data volumes.

CLOUD EMPOWERMENT

- **Real-time Insights:** It enables real-time data analysis and decision-making.
- **Cost-Efficiency:** Cloud resources can be provisioned and scaled on-demand, optimizing costs.

2. IOT PLATFORMS:

DESCRIPTION:

IoT platforms are all-encompassing solutions that make it easier to create, deploy, and manage applications and devices that are connected to the internet of things. These platforms give users access to essential services such as device management, data ingestion, security, and analytics.

Components of IoT Platforms:

- **Device Management:** Provisioning, monitoring, and managing IoT devices remotely.
- **Data Ingestion:** Collecting and storing data from devices in a structured format.
- **Security:** Ensuring data privacy, device authentication, and secure communication.
- **Analytics:** Processing and analyzing data to derive insights and make decisions.
- **Application Development:** Tools and APIs for building custom IoT applications.
- **Integration:** Integration with other cloud services and third-party applications.

UC 8.3: USE CASE TITLE- UTILIZING AN IOT PLATFORM TO MANAGE IOT ECOSYSTEM.

IoT devices are installed on the machines that a manufacturer of industrial equipment uses to monitor performance and reduce the likelihood of breakdowns. They manage their Internet of Things ecosystem with the help of an Internet of Things platform:

- **Device Management:** The platform gives the manufacturer the ability to remotely monitor the health of their machines, install firmware updates, and troubleshoot issues without having to send technicians to the location where the machines are located.
- **Ingestion of Data:** Information collected by sensors mounted on machines is taken in by the platform and filed away in a time-series database for later use in performing historical research.
- **Security** is ensured by the platform by encrypting data while it is being transmitted and restricting access to and control of the machines to only those individuals who have been granted permission to do so.
- **Analytics:** The platform contains algorithms for predictive maintenance, which examine sensor data in order to identify the early warning signs of a machine failing. When abnormalities are found, alerts for maintenance are sent to the relevant technicians.
- **Application Development:** The manufacturer builds a custom dashboard by utilizing the platform's application programming interfaces (APIs). This dashboard displays real-time data on the performance of the machine as well as maintenance schedules.

Benefits of IoT Platforms:

- Rapid Development: IoT platforms accelerate the development of IoT solutions, reducing time-to-market.
- Scalability: They are designed to scale as the number of IoT devices grows.
- Security: Built-in security features help protect IoT ecosystems from vulnerabilities.

In conclusion, the combination of IoT and cloud technologies makes it possible for businesses to harness the power of the data and devices that are connected to their networks. IoT architecture is what specifies how data moves between devices and the cloud, while IoT platforms are what supply the tools and services required for effective IoT ecosystem management. This synergy is causing industries to undergo transformation by making real-time insights, automation, and improved decision-making possible.

8.3. MACHINE LEARNING AND AI IN THE CLOUD

Machine Learning (ML) and Artificial Intelligence (AI) in the cloud have evolved into indispensable resources for businesses that want to capitalize on data-driven insights and intelligent automation. Machine learning services, artificial intelligence models and application programming interfaces are some of the AI and ML services that cloud providers offer. Let's look at some real-world examples of each of these.

1. MACHINE LEARNING SERVICES:

DESCRIPTION:
Machine learning services in the cloud provide a platform for building, training, and deploying machine learning models without the need to manage the underlying infrastructure. These services offer tools and libraries for data preparation, model training, and model deployment.

UC 8.4: USE CASE TITLE- MACHINE LEARNING SERVICES

Imagine for a moment that a company that offers online shopping wants to offer more personalized product recommendations to its clients. In

171

order to construct a recommendation engine, they make use of the machine learning services offered by a cloud provider (such as Amazon Web Services, Microsoft Azure, or Google Cloud), namely:

- **Data Preparation:** In order to prepare the data, the company collects information on customers' browsing histories, purchase histories, and interactions with products. They clean the data and then transform it into a format that can be used for training by using data processing tools that are hosted in the cloud.

- **Model Training:** The company offers machine learning services, and as part of those services, it develops recommendation algorithms by using libraries such as TensorFlow or PyTorch. They use data from the past to train the model, which then learns to make educated guesses about the kinds of products a particular customer is likely to buy based on that customer's past purchasing patterns.

- **Deployment of the Model:** Once the model has been trained, it is either deployed in the form of an API or integrated into the website of the company. When a customer visits the website, the model immediately provides them with individualized recommendations for products to purchase.

Benefits of Machine Learning Services:

- Ease of Use: Organizations can leverage machine learning without needing extensive ML expertise.
- Scalability: Cloud services can handle large-scale data and model training.
- Cost Efficiency: Pay-as-you-go pricing models reduce infrastructure costs.

2. AI MODELS AND APIS:

Description:

AI models and application programming interfaces (APIs) in the cloud offer pre-trained machine learning models and APIs for specific AI tasks.

CLOUD EMPOWERMENT

These tasks include natural language processing (NLP), computer vision, and speech recognition. These models require very little configuration and are ready to use right out of the box.

UC 8.5: USE CASE TITLE- AI MODELS AND API

Take, for example, a healthcare organization with the goal of gleaning useful information from patients' medical records through the application of natural language processing. They make use of the AI models and APIs that are made available by a cloud provider:

- **Text Extraction:** The organization uploads medical records in text format to the cloud service.
- **AI Model:** The cloud AI service includes a pre-trained NLP model that can extract medical entities like patient names, diagnoses, and treatments from the text.
- **API Integration:** The organization integrates the AI API into their workflow. When new medical records are uploaded, the API automatically extracts relevant information.
- **Insights:** The extracted data is used to generate insights, such as disease prevalence, treatment trends, and patient outcomes.

Benefits of AI Models and APIs:

- **Rapid Deployment:** Organizations can quickly implement AI capabilities without extensive model training.
- **Accuracy:** Pre-trained models benefit from large datasets and robust training, resulting in accurate predictions.
- **Broad Applicability:** Cloud providers offer APIs for a wide range of AI tasks, from image recognition to language translation.

Machine learning and artificial intelligence hosted in the cloud give businesses the ability to leverage the power of data-driven insights and intelligent automation. While machine learning services make it possible

173

to develop, train, and deploy custom models, artificial intelligence models and application programming interfaces (APIs) provide pre-trained models that are tailored to a variety of tasks. These cloud-based solutions democratize artificial intelligence (AI) by making it available to businesses of any size, which in turn drives innovation and improves decision-making across a variety of industries.

Chapter 9:
Cloud Trends and Future Outlook

9.1. EMERGING CLOUD TECHNOLOGIES

The landscape of cloud computing is continuously being reshaped by emerging cloud technologies, which offer new capabilities and opportunities for organizations. The integration of quantum computing with the cloud, edge computing, and advancements in serverless computing are three notable examples of new cloud technologies that are currently in development. In order to better understand each of these, let's look at some examples.

1. EDGE COMPUTING:

Description:
Edge computing is a paradigm of distributed computing that moves computation and data storage closer to the data source (Internet of Things devices, sensors, and so on). This brings latency down and improves real-time processing. Edge computing is also known as fog computing. Cloud computing is extended to the edge of the network through edge computing, which enables faster response times and more efficient data processing. Edge computing is an extension of cloud computing.

UC 9.1: USE CASE TITLE- AUTONOMOUS VEHICLES

Think about driverless cars that are loaded up with a ton of different sensors and cameras. These vehicles produce enormous amounts of data, which needs to be processed very quickly in order to make decisions regarding driving in real time. The following is an example of an appropriate application for edge computing:

- **Data Processing at the Edge:** Each autonomous vehicle is outfitted with computing devices at the edge of the network (edge servers or edge nodes). These devices process sensor data locally and make instant decisions regarding steering, acceleration, and braking without waiting for the data to be sent to a centralized cloud server. These decisions can be made in real time.
- **Reduced Latency:** Processing data at the edge significantly reduces latency, which enables vehicles to respond in milliseconds to changing road conditions or obstacles.
- **Cloud Integration:** While crucial decisions regarding the system's safety are made at the edge, less time-sensitive data (such as historical data or software updates, for example) can still be transmitted to the cloud for the purposes of conducting long-term analysis and making improvements.

Benefits of Edge Computing:

- Low Latency: Edge computing reduces latency, making it ideal for applications requiring real-time processing.
- Bandwidth Savings: Less data needs to be transmitted to the cloud, reducing bandwidth usage and costs.
- Resilience: Edge computing systems can operate autonomously, even when the cloud connection is lost.

2. SERVERLESS COMPUTING

DESCRIPTION:

Serverless computing is a model of cloud computing in which code is written by developers in the form of functions or microservices, and the infrastructure, scaling, and resource allocation are all automatically managed by the cloud provider. Recent developments in serverless computing have resulted in increased flexibility and capability.

UC 9.2: USE CASE TITLE- MEDIA PROCESSING

Imagine a media streaming service that must convert videos into a number of different formats in order to support a variety of different types of devices. The following are some applications of serverless computing advancements:

- **Dynamic Scaling:** Recent developments in serverless platforms have made it possible to automatically scale the functions of media processing in response to changes in demand. When there are many users streaming videos, the service can quickly spawn additional transcoding instances to handle the load. During times when there are fewer users streaming videos, the service can scale down to save money.

- **Event-Driven Processing:** Events, such as the uploading of a new video file, can set off serverless functions to perform their work. The uploading of a video will begin the transcoding process because an event will cause a serverless function to be triggered.

- **Cost Optimization:** Serverless platforms provide fine-grained billing, which means that the streaming service only has to pay for the computing resources that are actually used during the video transcoding process. This helps to keep costs down.

Benefits of Serverless Computing Advancements:

- **Scalability** refers to the ability of serverless platforms to automatically scale up when activity levels are high and scale down when activity levels are low.

177

☁ **Pay-as-you-go** pricing, also known as pay-per-use pricing, is an effective method for lowering infrastructure expenses.

☁ **Development** is made easier because developers are able to concentrate on writing code rather than managing infrastructure.

3. QUANTUM COMPUTING AND THE CLOUD:

DESCRIPTION:

Quantum computing is a relatively new area of study that makes use of quantum bits, also known as qubits, to carry out calculations that are far too complicated for traditional computers to handle. The combination of cloud computing and quantum computing enables businesses to gain access to the processing power of quantum computers as a cloud service.

UC 9.3: USE CASE TITLE- CRYPTOGRAPHY AND SECURITY:

Traditional cryptographic algorithms can be broken using quantum computing, which leaves data open to intrusion from malicious parties. On the flip side, it can also improve security by helping to develop encryption methods that are resistant to quantum computing. The cloud has an essential part to play in the process of democratizing quantum cryptography:

☁ **Secure Data Transmission:** Quantum key distribution, also known as QKD, is a method that applies the concepts of quantum physics in order to ensure the safety of the exchange of encryption keys between companies. In order to improve the safety of data transmission, cloud providers may provide QKD as a service to their customers.

☁ **Quantum Simulations:** The capability of quantum computers to simulate complex quantum systems is useful in a wide variety of fields, including the study of materials, the search for new drugs, and the modeling of climate. Through the utilization of cloud-based quantum simulators, it is possible to provide researchers and businesses with access to the capabilities of quantum computing.

Benefits of Quantum Computing in the Cloud:

- Access to Quantum Power: Organizations can harness the computational capabilities of quantum computers without investing in specialized hardware.
- Enhanced Security: Quantum cryptography and encryption methods can provide more robust security for data transmission and storage.
- Scientific Advancements: Quantum computing in the cloud can accelerate research in quantum chemistry, physics, and materials science.

Emerging cloud technologies, such as serverless computing advancements and quantum computing integration, are pushing the boundaries of what is possible in the cloud. Examples of these technologies include edge computing and quantum computing. They provide businesses with new opportunities for real-time processing, cost-effective computing, and access to cutting-edge quantum capabilities, thereby opening doors to innovation and efficiency across a variety of different industries.

9.2. INDUSTRY USE CASES

CASE STUDIES AND SUCCESS STORIES

The real-world impact that cloud technologies have had in a variety of fields can be seen in the use cases and success stories that come from a variety of different industries. Take a look at the following use cases and success stories that are unique to a certain sector:

1. HEALTHCARE INDUSTRY:

UC 9.4: TELEMEDICINE AND REMOTE PATIENT MONITORING

Description: Cloud computing enables telemedicine platforms, which in turn enable healthcare providers to offer remote consultations and monitor patients' health using wearable devices in real time. During the COVID-19 pandemic, this use case came to the forefront of attention.

Example Success Story:

Teladoc Health: Cloud services are essential to the operation of the industry-leading telehealth service provider Teladoc Health. Teladoc experienced a significant rise in the number of users during the pandemic, reaching over 10 million virtual visits in the year 2020. They were able to smoothly manage the increase in demand thanks to the scalability provided by the cloud, which ensured that patients received timely care.

2. FINANCIAL SERVICES INDUSTRY:

UC 9.5: FRAUD DETECTION AND PREVENTION

Description: For the purpose of detecting and preventing fraud in real time, financial institutions utilize machine learning and data analytics that are cloud-based. They examine the data of transactions to look for unusual patterns and telltale signs of fraud.

Example Success Story:

Capital One: A major provider of financial services, Capital One, uses the cloud services offered by Amazon Web Services (AWS) for its fraud detection systems. They were successful in lowering the number of false positives, improving their ability to identify fraudulent activity, and providing efficient account protection for their customers.

CLOUD EMPOWERMENT

3. RETAIL INDUSTRY:

UC 9.6: Inventory Management and Demand FORECASTING

Description: Cloud-based analytics are used by retailers to optimize inventory levels, forecast customer demand, and reduce the likelihood of stockouts and excess inventory. Cloud-based analytics are also used to optimize inventory levels. This contributes to an increase in overall customer satisfaction, which, in turn, helps to reduce overall carrying costs.

Example Success Story:

Walmart: Cloud services provided by Microsoft Azure are leveraged by Walmart to manage its supply chain and inventory. Walmart is able to accurately forecast customer demand, optimize inventory across its thousands of stores, and reduce waste while simultaneously ensuring that products are readily available for customers because the company analyzes vast amounts of data.

4. MANUFACTURING INDUSTRY:

UC 9.7: PREDICTIVE MAINTENANCE

Description: In order for manufacturers to anticipate when their machinery will require maintenance, they use IoT devices and cloud analytics. Because of this, unplanned downtime is cut down, maintenance costs are reduced, and production efficiencies are improved.

EXAMPLE SUCCESS STORY:

Siemens: A cloud-based predictive maintenance system was implemented for Siemens' gas turbines, making the company a global leader in the manufacturing industry. Siemens is able to anticipate potential failures and schedule preventative maintenance for turbines thanks to the company's analysis of sensor data. Because of this, their customers have benefited from significant cost reductions as well as increased reliability.

5. ENTERTAINMENT INDUSTRY:

UC 9.8: CONTENT STREAMING AND PERSONALIZATION

Description: Streaming platforms make use of cloud infrastructure to expeditiously deliver content to users and to personalize content recommendations based on the actions and preferences of individual users.

Example Success Story:

Netflix: Netflix is an excellent illustration of a company that bases its entire infrastructure on cloud technology and relies on it exclusively. They stream content to millions of viewers all over the world by using the Amazon Web Services (AWS) platform. Additionally, in order to personalize content recommendations for each user, their recommendation algorithm makes use of machine learning that is performed in the cloud.

6. EDUCATION INDUSTRY:

UC 9.9: ONLINE LEARNING AND COLLABORATION

Description: Cloud-based platforms are being adopted by educational institutions for the purposes of online learning, collaboration, and data storage. The use of cloud computing enables seamless access to a variety of educational resources from any location.

EXAMPLE SUCCESS STORY:

Coursera: The cloud computing infrastructure is what allows the online learning platform Coursera to provide its courses to millions of students all over the world. Students will always have unhindered access to all of the educational materials and content that they need thanks to the scalability and dependability of cloud services.

7. TRANSPORTATION AND LOGISTICS INDUSTRY:

UC 9.10: ROUTE OPTIMIZATION AND ASSET TRACKING

Description: Cloud-based systems are utilized by companies in the transportation industry to facilitate route optimization, the monitoring of vehicle and cargo locations, and the improvement of fuel efficiency.

EXAMPLE SUCCESS STORY:

UPS: In order to streamline its business operations, UPS uses logistics and route optimization systems that are hosted in the cloud. UPS is able to improve overall efficiency, optimize delivery routes, and reduce fuel consumption by collecting data from sensors and GPS devices installed on its vehicles and analyzing that data.

These use cases and success stories from various industries demonstrate the disruptive impact that cloud technologies are having in a variety of different fields. They demonstrate how cloud solutions can improve operational efficiency, lower costs, and drive innovation, which will ultimately lead to improved customer experiences and increased business growth.

Chapter 10:
Conclusion and Resources

10.1. RECAP OF KEY POINTS

The all-encompassing cloud computing platform incorporates a wide variety of ideas, services, and software programs that are indispensable in the modern digital environment. A quick review of the most important points follows:

1. *CLOUD DEPLOYMENT MODELS:*

- **Public Cloud:** Services are hosted and managed by third-party providers, accessible over the internet. Examples include AWS, Azure, and Google Cloud.
- **Private Cloud:** Resources are dedicated to a single organization, providing more control and security. It can be on-premises or hosted by a third-party.
- **Hybrid Cloud:** Combines public and private clouds, allowing data and applications to move between them. Useful for scaling and data control.
- **Multi-Cloud:** Utilizing multiple cloud providers to avoid vendor lock-in, enhance redundancy, and optimize costs.

2. *DATA CENTERS AND SERVER FARMS:*

- **Data Center Architecture:** Facilities housing servers, storage, and networking equipment. May be on-premises or hosted by cloud providers.
- **Virtualization:** The process of creating virtual versions of resources (servers, storage, networks) to optimize utilization and resource allocation.

CLOUD EMPOWERMENT

3. NETWORKING IN THE CLOUD:

- **Virtual Private Cloud (VPC):** Isolates cloud resources logically, providing network security and segmentation.
- **Content Delivery Networks (CDNs):** Distribute content globally to improve website and application performance.
- **Network Security Groups (NSGs):** Control inbound and outbound traffic to and from cloud resources.

4. CLOUD USE CASES:

- **VPC Use Cases:** Securely hosting applications, creating isolated development environments, and enabling secure on-premises-to-cloud communication.
- **CDN Use Cases:** Speeding up website performance, delivering high-quality video streaming, and mitigating DDoS attacks.
- **NSG Use Cases:** Enforcing network security policies, segmenting network traffic, and protecting virtual machines and applications.

5. STORAGE IN THE CLOUD:

- **Object Storage:** Stores unstructured data as objects, suitable for backups, data lakes, and media storage.
- **Block Storage:** Provides raw storage volumes for use with virtual machines and databases.
- **File Storage:** Offers shared file systems for network-attached storage and file sharing.

6. COMPUTE RESOURCES IN THE CLOUD:

- **Virtual Machines (VMs):** Emulate physical computers and are suitable for running various applications and operating systems.
- **Containers and Kubernetes:** Isolate and run applications in lightweight containers, often managed with Kubernetes for orchestration.

☁ **Serverless Computing:** Allows developers to run code without managing servers, automatically scaling based on demand.

7. MAJOR CLOUD PROVIDERS:

☁ **Amazon Web Services (AWS):** Offers a vast array of cloud services, including computing, storage, databases, AI/ML, and more.

☁ **Microsoft Azure:** Provides a comprehensive suite of cloud services, especially popular among enterprises.

☁ **Google Cloud Platform (GCP):** Known for its data analytics, machine learning, and AI capabilities.

8. CLOUD MANAGEMENT TOOLS:

☁ **AWS Management Console:** AWS's web-based interface for managing cloud resources.

☁ **Azure Portal:** Microsoft's web portal for managing Azure services.

☁ **Google Cloud Console:** GCP's web-based interface for cloud management.

9. CLOUD COST MANAGEMENT:

☁ **Billing Models:** Pay-as-you-go, Reserved Instances (RIs), and Spot Instances offer flexibility and cost control.

☁ **Cost Optimization Strategies:** Right-sizing resources, tagging and resource grouping, and using cost monitoring tools to reduce cloud costs.

10. CLOUD MIGRATION STRATEGIES:

☁ **Lift and Shift:** Migrating existing applications to the cloud without major code changes.

☁ **Re-platforming:** Adapting applications to use cloud-native services and features.

☁ **Re-factoring:** Rewriting or redesigning applications to be cloud-native from the ground up.

CLOUD EMPOWERMENT

11. *CLOUD ADOPTION BEST PRACTICES:*

- **Change Management:** Preparing teams for cloud adoption, including training and cultural adjustments.
- **Training and Upskilling:** Investing in cloud training and upskilling to ensure a skilled workforce.

12. *BIG DATA AND ANALYTICS IN THE CLOUD:*

- **Data Lakes and Data Warehouses:** Storing and analyzing large volumes of data efficiently.
- **Analytics Services:** Leveraging cloud-based tools and services for data analysis, machine learning, and business intelligence.

13. *EMERGING CLOUD TECHNOLOGIES:*

- **Edge Computing:** Bringing computation closer to data sources for reduced latency and real-time processing.
- **Serverless Computing Advancements:** Enhanced scalability, event-driven computing, and cost-effectiveness.
- **Quantum Computing and the Cloud:** Integrating quantum computing power into cloud services for advanced calculations and security.

Comprehensive Cloud Technology is a field that is both dynamic and evolving, and it continues to be a driver of innovation and transformation across industries. It provides scalability, agility, and cost-efficiency to organizations all over the world.

10.2. FURTHER LEARNING RESOURCES

Certainly! Here is a list of further learning resources, including books, courses, and websites, to help you delve deeper into comprehensive cloud technologies:

BOOKS:

1. **"AWS Certified Solutions Architect Study Guide"** by Ben Piper, David Clinton, and Joseph Phillips. A comprehensive guide for preparing for the AWS Certified Solutions Architect certification.
2. **"Azure Essentials"** by Michael Collier and Robin Shahan. An introduction to Microsoft Azure, covering its core services and concepts.
3. **"Google Cloud Platform in Action"** by Dan McGrath, JJ Geewax, and Francis Bonnin-A hands-on guide to Google Cloud Platform, with practical examples and use cases.
4. **"Cloud Computing:** From Beginning to End" by Ray J. Rafaels: Offers a broad overview of cloud computing concepts, services, and deployment models.

ONLINE COURSES AND TUTORIALS:

1. **Coursera (Cloud Specializations):** Coursera offers various cloud-related specializations, including "Google Cloud Professional Cloud Architect" and "AWS Certified Solutions Architect."
2. **edX (Cloud Computing Courses):** edX provides courses on cloud computing from universities and institutions worldwide.
3. **Udemy (Cloud Courses):** Udemy offers a wide range of courses on AWS, Azure, Google Cloud, and cloud-related technologies.
4. **A Cloud Guru:** Offers hands-on training for AWS, Azure, Google Cloud, and other cloud platforms.

WEBSITES AND BLOGS:

1. **Cloud Academy:** Provides learning paths, hands-on labs, and quizzes on cloud technologies.
2. **AWS Blog:** Official blog from Amazon Web Services, featuring articles on AWS services and best practices.
3. **Azure Blog:** Microsoft's official blog for Azure, with updates, case studies, and tutorials.

4. **Google Cloud Blog:** Google Cloud's blog with articles on GCP services, customer stories, and industry insights.

5. **The Cloud Foundation:** A nonprofit organization dedicated to advancing cloud education, with resources and learning materials.

YOUTUBE CHANNELS:

1. **AWS YouTube Channel:** Official YouTube channel of Amazon Web Services, featuring tutorials, webinars, and customer success stories.

2. **Microsoft Azure YouTube Channel:** Azure's official YouTube channel with videos on Azure services and solutions.

3. **Google Cloud Platform YouTube Channel:** GCP's official YouTube channel, offering tutorials, tech talks, and product demos.

FORUMS AND COMMUNITIES:

1. **Stack Overflow:** A popular platform to ask and answer technical questions related to cloud technologies.

2. **Reddit Cloud Computing Community:** A subreddit dedicated to discussions on cloud computing.

3. **Cloud Computing on LinkedIn:** Join LinkedIn groups related to cloud computing to network and stay updated on industry trends.

It doesn't matter if you prefer books, online courses, blogs, or interactive platforms; these resources cover a broad spectrum of cloud technologies and are tailored to different learning styles. Because cloud computing is a rapidly developing field, it is essential to ensure that you are always abreast of the most recent advancements in the field.

10.3. CERTIFICATION PROGRAMS

Certification programs offered by Amazon Web Services (AWS), Microsoft Azure, and Google Cloud Platform (GCP) are highly respected in the IT industry. These certifications validate your cloud computing skills and knowledge, and they can significantly enhance your career prospects. Here's an overview of the certification programs offered by AWS, Azure, and GCP:

AMAZON WEB SERVICES (AWS) CERTIFICATIONS:

AWS offers a comprehensive certification program covering various skill levels and domains:

1. **AWS Certified Cloud Practitioner:**

- Level: Foundational
- Target Audience: Beginners, non-technical stakeholders
- Description: This certification introduces you to the basics of AWS, cloud concepts, services, and the AWS Well-Architected Framework.
- Example Exam Topics: Cloud concepts, AWS services overview, billing and pricing, security and compliance.

2. **AWS Certified Solutions Architect - Associate:**

- Level: Associate
- Target Audience: Solution architects, developers
- Description: Focuses on designing distributed systems on AWS, understanding architectural best practices, and selecting appropriate AWS services for specific use cases.
- Example Exam Topics: Designing highly available and scalable systems, choosing reliable and cost-effective storage solutions, securing applications and data.

3. **AWS Certified Developer - Associate:**

- Level: Associate

CLOUD EMPOWERMENT

- Target Audience: Developers, software engineers
- Description: Emphasizes developing and deploying applications on AWS, including writing code and interacting with AWS services through SDKs and APIs.
- Example Exam Topics: Developing AWS applications, understanding AWS services integration, security and best practices.

4. **AWS Certified SysOps Administrator - Associate:**

- Level: Associate
- Target Audience: System administrators, operations professionals
- Description: Focuses on managing and operating systems on AWS, covering areas like monitoring, deployment, and troubleshooting.
- Example Exam Topics: Systems operations on AWS, managing resources, automating tasks, and optimizing performance.

5. **AWS Certified Solutions Architect - Professional:**

- Level: Professional
- Target Audience: Experienced solution architects
- Description: An advanced certification that delves deeper into architectural design principles and best practices, including large-scale distributed systems.
- Example Exam Topics: Designing highly available, cost-efficient, fault-tolerant, and scalable systems.

6. **AWS Certified DevOps Engineer - Professional:**

- Level: Professional
- Target Audience: DevOps professionals, system administrators

- Description: Focuses on DevOps practices, including continuous delivery, automation, and security, in the context of AWS services.
- Example Exam Topics: Implementing and managing continuous delivery systems, monitoring and logging, security, and governance.

7. **AWS Certified Security - Specialty:**

- Level: Specialty
- Target Audience: Security professionals
- Description: This certification validates your expertise in securing AWS workloads and understanding security best practices.
- Example Exam Topics: Identity and access management, encryption, incident response, and security best practices.

8. **AWS Certified Data Analytics - Specialty:**

- Level: Specialty
- Target Audience: Data analysts, data engineers
- Description: Focuses on using AWS services for data analytics, including data collection, processing, and visualization.
- Example Exam Topics: Data collection, data storage, data processing, data analysis, and visualization.

9. **AWS Certified Machine Learning - Specialty:**

- Level: Specialty
- Target Audience: Machine learning practitioners, data scientists
- Description: Validates your machine learning knowledge and skills on AWS, covering ML models, data preparation, and deployment.
- Example Exam Topics: Data engineering, feature engineering, model training, model deployment, and ML best practices.

10. **AWS Certified Advanced Networking - Specialty:**

- Level: Specialty
- Target Audience: Network professionals

- Description: Focuses on advanced networking concepts and practices in AWS, including VPC design, hybrid connectivity, and network optimization.
- Example Exam Topics: Designing and implementing scalable AWS network architectures, optimizing network performance.

MICROSOFT AZURE CERTIFICATIONS:

Microsoft Azure offers a certification program with role-based certifications for various job roles:

1. **Microsoft Certified: Azure Fundamentals:**

- Level: Foundational
- Target Audience: Beginners, non-technical stakeholders
- Description: Introduces you to Azure cloud concepts, services, pricing, and basic cloud security.
- Example Exam Topics: Cloud concepts, Azure services, Azure pricing, and SLA.

2. **Microsoft Certified: Azure Administrator Associate:**

- Level: Associate
- Target Audience: Azure administrators, system administrators
- Description: Focuses on tasks related to managing Azure resources, implementing security, and ensuring efficient operations.
- Example Exam Topics: Managing Azure identities and governance, implementing and managing storage, configuring virtual networks, and monitoring and backup solutions.

3. **Microsoft Certified: Azure Developer Associate:**

- Level: Associate
- Target Audience: Azure developers, software engineers

- Description: Emphasizes developing solutions on Azure, including creating and optimizing Azure applications.
- Example Exam Topics: Developing Azure solutions, implementing Azure compute solutions, and developing for Azure storage.

4. **Microsoft Certified: Azure Solutions Architect Expert:**

- Level: Expert
- Target Audience: Solution architects, infrastructure architects
- Description: Covers advanced skills in designing and implementing solutions on Azure, including infrastructure and applications.
- Example Exam Topics: Designing for identity and security, designing a data platform solution, and designing for deployment, migration, and integration.

5. **Microsoft Certified: Azure DevOps Engineer Expert:**

- Level: Expert
- Target Audience: DevOps engineers, developers
- Description: Focuses on implementing DevOps practices, including continuous integration, continuous delivery, and automation, using Azure DevOps Services.
- Example Exam Topics: Implementing CI/CD pipelines, managing source control, and optimizing Azure DevOps performance.

6. **Microsoft Certified: Azure Security Engineer Associate:**

- Level: Associate
- Target Audience: Security professionals
- Description: Validates your expertise in securing Azure workloads and implementing security controls.
- Example Exam Topics: Managing identity and access, implementing platform protection, and managing security operations.

7. **Microsoft Certified: Azure AI Engineer Associate:**

CLOUD EMPOWERMENT

- Level: Associate
- Target Audience: AI engineers, data scientists
- Description: Focuses on using Azure AI services to build AI solutions, including machine learning models and natural language processing.
- Example Exam Topics: Developing AI solutions using Azure AI services, monitoring and optimizing models, and responsible AI.

8. **Microsoft Certified: Azure Data Scientist Associate:**

- Level: Associate
- Target Audience: Data scientists, AI professionals
- Description: Validates your skills in using Azure services for data science tasks, including data preparation, training models, and deployment.
- Example Exam Topics: Preparing data for analysis, building machine learning models, and deploying and managing models.

GOOGLE CLOUD PLATFORM (GCP) CERTIFICATIONS:

Google Cloud offers a certification program covering a range of GCP skills:

1. **Google Cloud Associate Cloud Engineer:**

- Level: Associate
- Target Audience: Beginners, cloud enthusiasts
- Description: Introduces you to GCP fundamentals, including managing GCP resources and services.
- Example Exam Topics: Setting up a cloud solution environment, planning and configuring a cloud solution, deploying and implementing a cloud solution.

2. **Google Cloud Professional Data Engineer:**

- Level: Professional
- Target Audience: Data engineers, data analysts
- Description: Focuses on designing data processing systems, data modeling, and data transformation on GCP.
- Example Exam Topics: Designing data processing systems, data preparation and exploration, machine learning and model evaluation.

3. **Google Cloud Professional Cloud Architect:**

- Level: Professional
- Target Audience: Solution architects, infrastructure architects
- Description: Covers advanced skills in designing scalable and reliable solutions on GCP.
- Example Exam Topics: Designing highly available, cost-effective, and secure solutions, managing and provisioning GCP resources.

4. **Google Cloud Professional Cloud DevOps Engineer:**

- Level: Professional
- Target Audience: DevOps engineers, developers
- Description: Focuses on continuous integration, continuous delivery (CI/CD), and site reliability engineering (SRE) practices on GCP.
- Example Exam Topics: Configuring CI/CD pipeline, monitoring and logging, and managing deployment infrastructure.

5. **Google Cloud Professional Machine Learning Engineer:**

- Level: Professional
- Target Audience: Machine learning engineers, data scientists
- Description: Emphasizes designing, building, and deploying machine learning models on GCP.
- Example Exam Topics: Model deployment, optimization, and prediction, data preparation and exploration, and building scalable ML models.

6. **Google Cloud Professional Cloud Security Engineer:**

- Level: Professional
- Target Audience: Security professionals, IT professionals
- Description: Validates your expertise in designing and managing security controls on GCP.
- Example Exam Topics: Configuring access within a cloud solution environment, configuring network security, and ensuring data protection.

7. **Google Cloud Professional Cloud Network Engineer:**

- Level: Professional
- Target Audience: Network engineers, cloud architects
- Description: Focuses on designing and implementing network solutions on GCP.
- Example Exam Topics: Designing a hybrid network, configuring cloud interconnect, and implementing VPNs.

These certification programs provide a structured path to acquire cloud skills, and each certification is designed for specific roles and skill levels in the cloud computing industry. Obtaining a cloud certification requires a certain level of expertise. A certain level of knowledge and experience is needed in order to become certified in cloud computing.

We can improve our career prospects, increase our earning potential, and demonstrate that we are expert in cloud technologies if anyone earns one or more of these certifications. These certifications can be earned individually or in combination. Consider earning at least one of these certifications if you want to be able to do all of those things; alternatively, consider earning all of them. It is of the utmost importance that you select the certifications that are aligned with the professional goals and areas of interest that you have for yourself.

It is essential knowledge to be aware of the fact that the technologies associated with cloud computing are continuously undergoing development. Because staying abreast of the most recent developments in the industry is of the utmost importance, it is strongly recommended that you use this manual as a foundational resource within your training program.

Appendices

HOW TO MANAGE TECH PROJECTS?

When it comes to embracing and utilizing cloud technology, non-tech business personnel may encounter a number of difficulties. While cloud computing has many advantages, it also poses some particular challenges for those without a strong technological experience. Here are some typical issues with cloud technology that non-technical business professionals may run into:

Complexity: Cloud technology can be intricate, making it difficult for non-tech experts to comprehend the specifics of cloud services, setups, and maintenance. They could have trouble understanding the technical terms and concepts.

Security Issues: Businesses have many security issues using the cloud. When their data is kept on the cloud, non-tech professionals could be concerned about data breaches, compliance issues, and the overall security of their data. It can be difficult to make sure that adequate security measures are in place.

Cost Control: Because cloud services sometimes use a pay-as-you-go business model, if costs are not adequately controlled, they can easily become out of hand. Non-technical professionals could find it difficult to monitor and manage their cloud spending.

Integration issues: It might be difficult to integrate current systems and applications with cloud services. Providing seamless connectivity between on-premises systems and cloud-based solutions may be challenging for non-tech personnel.

Lack of Technical Knowledge: Non-tech personnel might not possess the necessary technical expertise to efficiently resolve problems or optimize cloud resources. Inefficiencies and downtime may result from this.

Data Transfer and Migration: Moving applications and data to the cloud can be a labor-intensive and complicated procedure. Data loss or corruption may be a problem for non-tech professionals during data migration.

Vendor lock-in: It can be challenging and expensive to select a cloud service provider, then transfer providers. Non-tech professionals can feel constrained by the ecosystem of a specific provider, which would reduce their flexibility.

Reliability and downtime: Cloud services are not impervious to disruptions and downtime. Cloud service outages could cause corporate activities to be disrupted for non-tech workers.

Compliance and Regulations: Strict regulatory standards may apply to data management and storage, depending on the industry. It is the responsibility of non-tech professionals to make sure that their cloud solutions abide by these rules.

Training and education: It might be difficult to keep up with the rapidly changing world of cloud computing. Non-technical workers might need to spend time and money on education and training in order to stay informed and make wise decisions.

Non-technical business professionals may want to collaborate with cloud technology specialists in IT to address these obstacles. Additionally, investing in cloud management tools and training courses will help them gain a better grasp of how to use cloud resources efficiently while minimizing potential issues.

If you adopt the right strategy and are willing to learn, you may manage technology projects for your organization even if you are not an engineer or did not complete a technology program. Non-technical managers have been shown to be reluctant and lacking in confidence when accepting duties involving technology.

The following is an in-depth walkthrough of the most efficient way to manage technological projects:

CLOUD EMPOWERMENT

Acquire a Solid Understanding of the Project's Aims and Prerequisites:

To get started, begin by articulating the project's objectives, goals, and needs in a language that is not technical. Which challenge are you attempting to overcome? What are the results that should be expected?

Create a Team That Is Capable:

Put together a group of people who have the appropriate level of technical expertise. In this context, "hiring tech experts" could also mean working along with existing staff members who already possess the necessary skills.

Study the Fundamentals:

It's not necessary for you to be a tech whiz, but it is essential that you have at least a fundamental awareness of the technologies that are involved in your project. Make an investment of some of your time to educate yourself about the technology, tools, and processes that are pertinent to your project.

The Importance of Communication

It is essential to have effective communication. Make sure that everyone on your team as well as any stakeholders understands the goals, timelines, and expectations of the project. Encourage communication that is both open and on a regular basis in order to answer issues and concerns.

The Planning of Projects:

Create a comprehensive strategy for the project that outlines all of the tasks, dates, milestones, and dependencies involved. The implementation of the project will be guided by this plan in the form of a roadmap.

Management of the Budget:

Create and maintain a budget for the project by working closely with the department in charge of your company's finances. Keep an eye on the spending, and make sure the project doesn't go over its allotted budget.

Administration of Risk:

Determine what the potential dangers are and then draft a plan to deal with them. This should include plans for minimizing potential dangers and resolving problems when they crop up.

Monitoring and Reporting on the Project:

Install tools and software for project management, and use them to keep track of progress, organize tasks, and generate reports. Helpful applications include Trello, Asana, and Microsoft Project, among others.

The Assurance of Quality:

Maintain a high level of focus on quality assurance and testing throughout the lifecycle of the project. Ensure that the finished product satisfies the quality criteria that have been established.

Administration of Vendors and Contractors:

When working with outside suppliers or contractors, it is important to draw up detailed contracts and lay out your expectations. Maintain consistent communication with them to ensure that they are fulfilling the criteria of the project.

Maintain an Awareness:

Educate yourself consistently on the technological aspects of the project as well as the general tendencies in the sector. Participate in conferences, webinars, and workshops to keep yourself current.

Ability to adjust:

Maintain a flexible mindset and a willingness to make necessary adjustments. Technology initiatives frequently undergo changes, and maintaining an adaptable mindset can help produce superior results.

Providing Documentation:

It is essential to keep detailed documentation of the project, including project plans, meeting minutes, and any relevant technical material. This will be helpful for references as well as for projects in the future.

Responses and assessments:

After the project has been finished, it is important to collect feedback from the team and the stakeholders. Evaluate the success of the project

CLOUD EMPOWERMENT

in comparison to the initial objectives, and locate areas in which it could be improved.

Improvement That Is Constant:

Make use of the knowledge gained from each project to strengthen your skills in project management and refine your procedures in preparation for future technological endeavors.

It is important to keep in mind that the successful administration of a project requires not only a high level of technical expertise but also strong leadership, communication, and organizational skills. Utilizing the abilities that members of your team possess and requesting assistance or direction when it is required can go a long way toward ensuring the successful management of technological initiatives.

AUTHOR'S NOTE

"**Cloud Empowerment**" is an approachable and user-friendly introduction to cloud technology that has been developed specifically for business professionals who are not technically savvy. This book provides readers with the knowledge and insights necessary to effectively harness the power of cloud computing in a world where cloud computing has become an integral part of modern business operations. In this world, the cloud has become an integral part of modern business operations.

Principal Attributes:

Dispelling Some Myths About the Cloud: This book simplifies a lot of difficult technical jargon and concepts into language that is straightforward and straightforward to understand. It gives readers a strong foundation in cloud technology without overburdening them with technical details, so they can make informed decisions.

Use Cases Derived from Real-World Applications: The book "Cloud Empowerment" presents a variety of practical use cases that illustrate how cloud computing can be utilized to improve a company's productivity and growth. These use cases span a variety of business sectors, illustrating the adaptability of cloud-based solutions.

Insights Into Strategic Implications: In addition to providing technical explanations, the book delves into the various strategic implications of adopting cloud technology. Readers gain a better understanding of the ways in which cloud technology can affect the competitiveness, scalability, and agility of their organizations.

Effective Cost Management: It is essential to have a solid understanding of cost management when working in the cloud. This book is an invaluable resource for companies that are looking to maximize their return on investment (ROI), as it provides actionable advice on how to maximize cloud spending.

CLOUD EMPOWERMENT

Concerns Regarding Cloud Security and Compliance: In this day and age of data breaches and stringent regulatory mandates, "Cloud Empowerment" addresses worries regarding cloud security and compliance. It offers advice on how to comply with applicable regulations while maintaining the security of data stored in the cloud.

The state of technology is one that is constantly undergoing change. The reader will be able to stay one step ahead of the curve and be better prepared for future developments by reading this book because it offers insights into emerging trends in cloud computing.

Takeaways That Can Be Put into Action: At the end of each chapter, the author provides readers with a set of takeaways that can be put into action right away in their businesses as well as some practical advice.

Audience:

"Cloud Empowerment" seeks to achieve the following goals:

Business Owners Entrepreneurs and business leaders who want to use cloud technology to improve their operations, cut costs, and drive growth in their businesses are considered business owners.

Managers: Managers working in a variety of departments, such as information technology (IT), finance, and marketing, who need to have an understanding of the potential impact that cloud technology could have on their teams.

Entrepreneurs: Founders and teams of startups that are looking to build scalable and cost-effective infrastructures from the ground up are the target audience for this solution.

Students and Teachers: Students and teachers who are interested in becoming professionals and teachers who are looking for a resource that is both comprehensive and easy to understand regarding cloud computing.

Why Should You Read About Cloud Empowerment?

In a world in which cloud technology is reshaping business landscapes and the industries that comprise them, "Cloud Empowerment" gives non-technical professionals the ability to tap into the transformative potential of this technology. This book is your essential guide to comprehending, implementing, and thriving in the cloud-driven era. Packed with real-world examples, strategic insights, and practical advice, this book is your go-to resource for all things cloud-related.

"Cloud Empowerment" will equip you with the knowledge and confidence to make informed decisions that can drive the success of your organization in the digital age, regardless of how long you've been in charge of a company or how recently you've begun exploring the possibilities offered by cloud technology. This is true regardless of whether you're an experienced business leader or someone who is just beginning to investigate the possibilities offered by cloud technology.

ABOUT THE AUTHOR

An esteemed Indo-Canadian author from the Indian state of Odisha, Sunil Das, has written **"Cloud Empowerment: *Demystifying Cloud Technology for Business Professionals*"** To include his additional works on Youth Empowerment, Compassionate Leadership, Science & Spirituality, and ,Philosophy.

This piece of writing clearly explains the complexities of cloud technology, with a focus on meeting the requirements of business professionals. Mr. Das's extensive and varied knowledge in the disciplines of technology, business, and education significantly contributes to the breadth of his written work.

Mr. Das's PMP, PMIBA SAFe 6.0, SAFe SPC, AWS and SNOWFLAKE credentials demonstrates his extensive knowledge and expertise in the field of business analysis, including the application of industry-leading methodologies and strategies along with his proficiency in implementing agile and lean methodologies at a larger scale, with the goal of fostering innovation and enhancing operational efficacy within large organizational structures.

Mr. Das's possesses master's degrees in both Physics and Management Information Systems with a strong passion for education, youth mentorship & Empowerment. This diversified educational background equips him with a unique blend of scientific and management expertise, allowing him to approach complex topics with a multifaceted approach.

Sunil has held positions in India, the United States, and Canada. He has worked in a variety of industries and markets, thereby diversifying his background. The individual's international experience has enabled them to adapt and innovate in a variety of organizational contexts. Throughout

207

his illustrious career, Sunil has contributed to numerous industries by utilizing his industry expertise.

Utilizing cloud-based solutions, Mr. Das's accomplishments in education and conventional energy have propelled digital transformation, operational efficiency, and sustainability. Sunil supports the use of cutting-edge technology to enhance patient care, including data security and efficacy. Mr. Das has been a pioneer in the use of technology in education, developing innovative and dynamic learning environments. Financial institutions have been strengthened by Sunil's data-driven decision-making and stringent security measures.

In addition to cloud migration, data analytics, technology integration, and higher education, Sunil is an expert in a variety of other fields. The individual has a unique propensity for simplifying complex technical concepts so that they are understandable and applicable to individuals without technical knowledge. This ability provides the fundamental foundation for the notion of "Cloud Empowerment."

Mr. Das demonstrates a profound passion for the study and practice of leadership and management, in addition to his notable technological and entrepreneurial accomplishments. The individual in question displays a high level of productivity in his writing endeavours, producing informative resources on a variety of topics, including technology. The purpose of these resources is to provide individuals and organizations with the knowledge and insights necessary for achieving success.

Mr. Das's numerous writings can be found in Amazon Books including "Cloud Empowerment," demonstrate his commitment to assisting individuals and organizations in adapting, evolving, and achieving success in a dynamic technology environment. The individual's passion for leadership, management, and technological resources is evident, establishing him as a respected expert in these domains.

REFERENCES

- Smith, John. "Cloud Computing 101: A Beginner's Guide." - https://opensudo.org/cloud-computing-101-a-beginners-guide-to-cloud-computing/
- Robinson, Jane. "The Business Value of Cloud Computing: Strategies for Success." [Book]
- AWS Cloud Security: Best Practices: https://www.datasciencecentral.com/aws-cloud-security-best-practices/
- "Cloud Cost Management: https://www.vmware.com/au/topics/glossary/content/cloud-cost-management.html#:~:text=Cloud%20cost%20management%20(also%20known,maximize%20cloud%20usage%20and%20efficiency.
- "Amazon Web Services (AWS) Case Studies." https://aws.amazon.com/gametech/customers/
- "Microsoft Azure Customer Stories." https://customers.microsoft.com/en-s/home?sq=&ff=&p=0
- "Regulatory Compliance in the Cloud: https://www.trendmicro.com/en_us/what-is/cloud-security/cloud-compliance.html
- https://www.crowdstrike.com/cybersecurity-101/cloud-security/cloud-compliance/
- The Cyber Risk Handbook: Creating and Measuring Effective Cybersecurity Capabilities. By Domenic Antonucci · 2017.

www.ingramcontent.com/pod-product-compliance
Lightning Source LLC
LaVergne TN
LVHW051229050326
832903LV00028B/2314

* 9 7 9 8 8 6 0 5 3 8 4 3 6 *